I0535066

The Price
and Other Stories from Sierra Leone

Edited by
Mohamed Combo Kamanda

Sierra Leonean Writers Series

The Price
and Other Stories from Sierra Leone
Copyright © 2012 by M.C. Kamanda (Editor)

ISBN: 978-9988-1-4753-2

Printed in Ghana

Sierra Leonean Writers Series
c/o Mallam O. & J. Enterprises
120 Kissy Road, Freetown, Sierra Leone
publisher@sl-writers-series.org /

Cover Design: Mallam O.

Table of Contents

Kamanda, ed. / The Price & Other Short Stories

INTRODUCTION

The Price and Other Short Stories from Sierra Leone is the first anthology of short stories to be published by SLWS. The genres and themes of the stories are wide ranging and entertaining and capture the diversity of Sierra Leone as well as the contexts and experiences of the writers.

The lead story, *The Price,* by Oumar Farouk Sesay, reflects on formal university education and the political and moral decadence of the story's setting. On the day of her graduation, the protagonist wonders whether the certificate, which symbolises her university education, could be equated to everything she had to put herself through:

> 'The degree certificate I was now holding was not only a certificate of academic achievement, but also a certificate of isolation. It was equivalent to the number of teachers, lecturers and businessmen I had gone to bed with to acquire it. It was also equivalent to the years of detachment and years of sojourn in a make- believe world…'

In her pursuit of western education, she had revolted against one fabric of her cultural tradition - the Bondo Society - through the help of 'the reformists' in her village, consequently severing links with her parentage and her cultural roots! Beyond this story's thematic relevance is the author's ability to transform the lead character from an outcast into a leader: someone who is admired and adored, but who at the same time recognises her personal failings and those of her society's and ends up inspiring a revolution against its leaders. Sesay's story represents the lives of university students who live in pretence and indicts corrupt politicians and lecturers who exploit vulnerable students like Zainab in the story.

In *A Strange Kind of Vacation*, Alimamy Rassin Kamara shows the dangers of boundless trust and faith in fetish and black magic. As the story unfolds, the reader finds out that 'the bulletproof vest' does not stand a chance against the fire power of an actual gun. Belief in the supernatural is very common in Sierra Leonean (indeed African) culture. You only have to watch some *Sollywood*[1] films or similar movies from the continent to make sense of this. Some common elements of the supernatural used in these films and the real world include cowries, talismans, horns and teeth of Africa's fiercest carnivores. Strangely enough, it is not only the so-called 'illiterate' people who believe in superstition; educated people like Kumrabai, who has achieved everything that characterises success by Sierra Leonean standards, become victims of temptation to acquire security, safety, protection against witchcraft, juju and gunshots:

> 'Alpha Gbessay scooped water and herbs and washed Kumrabai from head to toe. When he was satisfied Kumrabai was clean, he asked him to step out of the pot. …Satisfied, Alpha Gbessay loaded a gun with a live bullet…A loud noise broke the silence of the night as the bullet tore into Kumrabai's chest ripping both his heart and lungs.'

---

[1] *Sollywood* is the alias for Sierra Leone's home video industry; the coinage is patterned after *Hollywood* (the American film industry), *Bollywood* (the Indian film industry), *Lollywood* (the Pakistani film industry) and *Nollywood* (Nigeria's home video industry).

This story also explores the 'Social Security' system in Sierra Leone – the extended family. One advantage of the extended family system is shared responsibility among family members. Parents bring up their children in the hope that if they succeed in their adult lives, they will take over from them. This can take many forms and occur at different stages, ranging from the occasional sharing of meals with less successful family members, to taking over the entire responsibility of caring for whole families. In this story, Bampya, the hero, spends vacations at his sister and brother-in-law's family residence. After the holidays, he is sent away complete with a set of new school uniforms, school fees and some pocket money. Kamara in this story also strikes a good balance between sorrow and humour: the tragic death of Kumrabai clearly elicits bleakness, while the fun that Bampya gets from his numerous admirers of the opposite sex in his age group both bring a smile to the reader and take you down memory lane.

In *Family Affair*, Mohamed Sheriff reminds readers of the terrible effects of the rebel war on ordinary citizens. Mammy Nana, the lead character, had waited for this chance: the opportunity to pay back the murderers of her only grandchild. When that murderer is finally caught and brought to the village centre for payback time, Mammy Nana finds out to her dismay, that the culprit is her own son.

> "I look at my own son, I look in his eyes. I have never seen so much misery and remorse written on anyone's face as it was inscribed on my son's, but his crime was unforgivable."

This story's appeal resides in Sheriff's literary style as well as in the balance between suffering and wit. While we

3

sympathise with Mammy Nana for the problems she faces as a result of the rebel attack on her village, we are equally amused by the fact that the rebel leader on whom her community seeks to wreak vengeance is her own son, not an outsider. The irony is conspicuous. Every Sierra Leonean is bound to have been affected by the civil war and its consequences in one way or another, particularly the horrific atrocities it visited on their own kith and kin. Nevertheless, it is salutary that this human and personal story enhances our understanding of thorny and no less complex personal experiences of individuals coming to terms with their loss in post-war Sierra Leone. Sheriff's *Family Affair* succinctly achieves this goal.

Gbanabom's *Too Loud for a Soccer Match* clearly captures the strategy that was used by rebels of Revolutionary United Front to spring a surprise entry into Freetown upon the residents, members of the security apparatus and the governing elite at the time. The writer shows how the rebels craftily used the football metaphor to achieve their goal and does so in an entertaining and fluently written narrative.

"The Eagles are coming down to Freetown! I can't believe this."

"You better do; I understand that Gig gave the okay last night to the sports officials, and come to think about it, you should know about that. It has been arranged that the Kono team will come to Freetown today…

Just then the distant shout of exuberance drifted in with the wind, reverberating like the passion of the ocean tide crashing on concave banks.

"That," Mammy Felleh said, hesitating, "is too loud for a soccer match."

But, not even Mammy Felleh's scepticism was enough to derail the master plan of a rumour that has been meticulously planned and carefully executed, through the help of the rebel machinery —'insiders' who were already residing and doing the ground work in the city.

As well as the focus on the rebels' entry and subsequent massacre they caused, Gbanabom insightfully explores sub-themes as lechery, greed & self-aggrandisement, some of these portrayed either as bye-products of the social malaise that preceded the war, or as the immorality that usually fuels and characterise armed conflict. The appeal of this story lies in its thematic relevance in a country still reeling from the trauma of the war, the sincerity and depth with which some cultural nuances are explored, as well as the writer's craft of deploying familiar literary devices to achieve maximum effect. This is a gripping story!

Half a Pot Full by Karamoh Kabba, is a romantic comedy that recounts a father's treatment of his girl child, as if the latter is a piece of property. Arranged marriages are very common even in the 21st century; in some cultures a prospective suitor can engage a girl child at birth! Among the *Mende* for example, the bride gets to know about such arrangements at the very last minute, after graduating from the *Bondo society* - a rite of passage. This is how Dabuteh, the lead character in the story, finds out about her own bridegroom —to- be:

> 'Dabuteh had fastened her little fishing basket onto her head-tie…She came close to her father and said in a subtle voice, "Father, I want to go fishing with my mothers." She was mesmerised by the presence of two men.'

5

It turns out that one of these strange men is Dabuteh's suitor. Although he had been stopping over during his numerous trips to Kwendu, on this particular occasion, Alhaji appeared to have come prepared for the finale: he had brought gifts of clothes, food and lots of money. It is no surprise even to Dabuteh herself that after Alhaji departs, she is initiated into the rite of passage that signals readiness for marriage. This short story is a social comment on one of Sierra Leone's notorious cultural practice. It is fair to say that parents like Dabuteh's father are today facing challenges from an enlightened generation of girl children who refuse to marry their parents' choices of bridegrooms as well as openly protest against the torture of an ancient and barbaric traditional practice.

The title of the next story, *BackHomeAbroad by* Onipede Hollist, represents living abroad and being at home at the same time. The story's main setting is the United States of America. The hero, Foday, who holds a Master's degree and was former Assistant Secretary in the Ministry of Education, lives in the USA with his family. He does all kinds of low paid job for his family's basic survival. As well as finding money for his family's welfare, Foday has to cater for the numerous needs of the extended family at home. Living abroad has not offered him and his family any freedom from contact as he cannot avoid 'collect calls' made by members of his extended family, who believe they also have a claim on their son's finances. As well as reminding readers of the harsh impact of Sierra Leone's senseless war on families in the Diaspora, Hollist highlights some of the difficulties of interethnic marriage. Prior to the exchanges in the following passage from the story, the reader expects Foday, who is already unhappy about his wife's attitude

6

towards his parents, to take out his anger on his wife, Claudine. Unfortunately, it is Claudine who attacks Foday for taking money from her account without telling her:

> "Why did you take the money I had put aside to make the mortgage payment and not tell me?
> What did you do with it? What sort of behaviour is this?"
> The questions exploded in quick succession behind Foday's head like concussion grenades. The questions were from Claudine and she fired them off as she walked toward the kitchen before she appeared in Foday's peripheral vision.

Another appeal of this story lies in the subtlety with which Hollist revisits the familiar theme of culture clash, particularly the conflict between 'up line country people' versus the indigenous Creoles of the city. As well as this, there is the author's sophisticated use of language and literary devices which have the capacity to engage and entrance readers.

Removing the Veil by James Bernard Taylor, portrays a polygamous husband, Tamu, trying to strike a balance between his love for his bride, Yani, and his determination that she should give birth to a child. He spends a valuable proportion of the family's financial resources on improving Yani's chances of child-bearing through hiring a priest for cleansing her womb and for eliminating potential evil causes. The society portrayed in this story is truly a male-dominated one where a woman is blamed for everything, including the husband's inability to function effectively. If the wife refuses to comply, she could pay a heavy price, ranging from divorce to even death:

7

'Yani now lay almost naked on the floor with both
breasts exposed and her eyes closed… She groaned
and moaned as the priest sucked her breast for milk
like a hungry baby.'

This is one example of how Yani and her rivals experienced
humiliation throughout the cleansing ceremony. Such is the
power of Tamu that not even the priest can point an
accusing finger at him. How ironical that in the end, Yani's
chances of motherhood are improved not by the fetishism
that subjects her and her mates to indignation, but by the
intervention of health workers from the World Health
Organization. In this way, Taylor cleverly satirises the ills of
a macho culture strongly anchored in ignorance, poverty
and illiteracy.

The Dark Man by Brian James gives readers a glimpse of
gruesome aspects of Sierra Leone's traditional beliefs and
practices such as sacrificing an only male child in pursuit of
power. In this story, a naïve boy gets mysteriously separated
from his mother in a busy market place; he is later
surrounded and kidnapped by strange men. After what
seemed an endless period of captivity, his father arrives.

'At the moment a big man enters the clearing and
walks towards the fire. He is wearing a flowing blue
gown. Even before the flames light up his face, I
know from his walk that he is my father. My joy
knows no bounds …'

As well as the theme, there are other narrative hooks that
will thrill and excite the reader, such as the use of suspense.
The reader's sympathy for this boy is aroused more by the
child's innocence, faith and trust in his dubious father, who
exemplifies evil, than by the victim's fatal end.

8

Their Special Days by Frederick Borbor James is a snapshot of the youthful exuberance of five unmarried men. In addition to the luxury apartment they occupy, these young, energetic and enterprising university graduates can even afford to hire a caretaker for their domestic chores, making them the envy of their equals:

> 'Their lunch and dinner were prepared by the numerous fiancées and girlfriends that the men had.'

So, they had it all: a decent place to live, good jobs and the ultimate dream for many young men – beautiful women. One of the five men is distinct from the rest. His lack of interest in the opposite sex is perceived as an inadequacy. *'Could he be a eunuch?'* they wondered.
The method of disproving their suspicion is both farfetched and extravagant.

> "You are in for blackmail, so you have to comply."
> "What do you mean?"
> "They say you're not a man… I am here to prove them right or wrong…"

The appeal of this story lies in many factors, including the characteristic humour generated by the exploits of the bachelors and the effectiveness with which James brings the scenes and characters to life.

Wasted Trust by Mohamed Combo Kamanda also pokes fun at unlimited faith in Black Magic. In this story, Kamanda tries to ridicule the sort of trust that some people put in man-made forms of protection against evil and harm. The hero's fatal end is a consequence of this. There was a time in Sierra Leone when protection against gunshots was possible through the use of crudely constructed 'bullet proof vests'. Those were the days of the *Shakabula*, a locally made gun that misfired more often than not. Nowadays, the prevalence of the *Kalashnikov*, which is another terrible reminder of the rebel war, has both increased gun crime and more significantly made the 'bullet proof vest' irrelevant as Kenawa, the hero, discovers:

> 'As the kissing couple heard the gunshot zipping past, the woman scurried into the mansion to safety. One of the men turned fearfully in the direction of the shot's origin, gasping as he recognised the female figure that was still aiming another shot in their direction. He tried to duck but it was too late; three bullets in succession hit him on his chest. He fell dramatically, like a log on the cold wet tarmac.'

The effectiveness of this story lies in the crisp descriptive details of setting and character which brings them to life, as well as the writer's knowledge and experiences of the cultural and thematic issues explored, symbolised by the references to specific artefacts and concepts like *nyangobaa* (eclipse) and power of the *kaavaa* (traditional pen used by Islamic scholars).

If Ebenezer could Talk by Yema Lucilda Hunter is an absorbing story: sombre, solemn and thought-provoking. The narrator is a stroke victim who has been reduced to a helpless state: immobile but still mentally active… In his current state, Ebenezer only wishes he could reverse time, so he can still play the commanding role in directing the affairs of his family.

> 'Today is different. Jamesina is quiet after her usual greeting; sighs heavily between exercises, and even loses her rhythm from time to time. I wonder what is bothering her and try to ask, but as usual now, all that emerges from my lips is gibberish, even though

I am forming perfect sentences in my head. Tears of
frustration sting my eyes and trickle onto the pillow.'
To tell a story from the point of view of a speechless first
person narrator is a measure of Hunter's impressive literary
sophistication, richness of creativity and imagination. This
unique narrative style enriches and makes the story
outstanding. The reader is bound to feel sorry for Ebenezer,
whose past exploits and current state of inactivity are both
hugely contrasting and superbly appealing.

The Trap by Sheikh Umarr Kamara clearly captures one of
Sierra Leone's moral fables that a generation of older
readers would have heard recounted by their grandparents
around the firesides or dinner tables, long before the rebel
war came to the country's peaceful shores. This story was
first published by the *PEA* in *Fishing in the Rivers of Sierra
Leone* (Hinzen et al. eds. 1987). As well as maintaining the
original characters, Kamara's simple but captivating
narrative style is characteristic of the traditional folklore
genre. Take a look!

> 'One morning, just when Rat was getting ready to
> go to the garden, he saw Ya Yenoh setting up a trap
> on one of the potato beds. He watched from the
> nearby bush and realised that the garden had
> become dangerous for thieves. Rat stayed away
> from the garden for a couple of days. After debating
> in his mind what course to take, he concluded that
> he should meet the old woman's farm friends, Cow,
> Goat and Cock...'

The Trap offers a refreshing ending to the collection of short
stories from Sierra Leone. Being folkloric and intrinsically
Sierra Leonean, *The Trap* is bound to refresh, entertain and

educate the reader, like the rest of the short stories in this collection.

****

The expressed aim of the publisher of the **Sierra Leonean Writers Series** (SLWS) is to give every capable Sierra Leonean a chance to publish. *SLWS* is, more importantly, on an unstoppable mission to provide affordable and motivating books that will remedy the lack of suitable reading materials in schools, colleges, universities and the wider society. Publishing short stories in an anthology is another way of achieving this goal. The opportunity to be published is offered both to established and up-and-coming writers.

Oumar Farouk Sesay

THE PRICE

I stood alone among the teeming crowd. Perhaps I was the only graduate whose mood sharply contrasted with the festive mood at the Amphitheatre, where the graduates and well-wishers gathered to witness the conferment of degrees. A sea of smiling faces surrounded me. I wore an expression that looked like a combination of a smile and a frown, which I managed to produce with great effort. The turmoil inside me was capable of producing nothing other than a dissolute cry of anguish. I pretended to smile to appease the well-wishers who would have queried anything short of a smile on a day like that. I managed to maintain the smile like a statue in pain. Perhaps that is what I was, for only a statue could maintain a deadpan expression on such a day. Like a statue, I was absolutely detached from the general mood, so detached that I forgot I was one of the graduates until a friend jokingly said, "I shall be coming tonight for the convocation party."

His remark blasted me from my stupor, much like a cast member who is reminded of his or her lines in the middle of a performance.

"I will send you the invitation card for the party," I muttered, unsure of the compromise between my expression and my utterance.

"I will not wait for it", he replied.

He went into the rubble of the tower of Babel that had just collapsed around us. Congratulatory messages poured in

13

from groups of all sorts. They never wanted to know who you were; all they looked for was the academic gown for them to descend on you like bees on a honeycomb. Photographers hunted for these unique moments to take a snapshot because they know the pictures would be paid for either by the graduates or the well-wishers. I had already taken several snapshots with my mask-like face and it had started to bother me.

I began to move like driftwood in the ebb and flow of the human traffic. Others moved in search of friends, or to get the bus; yet, some members of the audience moved around to have a glimpse of the chancellor of the university who was also the president of Sumbuya. I had no intension of intimidating a friend with my mask-like face, nor did I desire to see the chancellor, whose hands I had already shaken when he invited me into the Bachelor of Arts degree second division. As I moved, the feeling of alienation dawned on me. I was the only graduate who was not flanked by parents. The temporary warmth provided by friends and well-wishers became a chilly reminder. When they embraced me, I thought of what it would have been to be embraced by my parents on this special day in my life.

But was it special? It ought to have been special because this day represented a summation of the sixteen good years of my life spent in drab classrooms and boarding homes. Perhaps this day summed up the life I had lived. It was special and ought to have been shared by those who planned it. I don't know if it was anger, feeling self-pity, or disappointment, but for some odd reason, I was propelled through the crowd in search of some safe quiet place, somewhere I could cry out my sadness, my empty heart. I found the spot by the statue of Kennedy at the Kennedy Building. After all, I was nothing other than a statue in pain. I sat by the statue and pondered.

I unfolded the paper in my hand; it was the certificate I have worked for in the past sixteen years of my earthly life. I read and reread it. The colourful print of the certificate suddenly disappeared, and in its place, a number of question marks appeared. Was this the price for all the years I had spent: relations severed, reputation stained, and abortions in shady clinics? Was this the price? I wanted to dismiss the question but it wasn't dismissible. Because in answering it, I explained the absence of my parents in the convocation, my sad mood, my alienation, and deep grief for the loss of Zainab, the only true friend I ever had all my life. Was this the price for the isolation I had suffered?

I recalled my first day at school. I was dragged from the hands of the *Soweis* (female leaders of the Bondo secret society) as they prepared me for the rite of passage into womanhood through initiation into the Bondo society. My proposed initiation into the Bondo society opened a debate about the merits and demerits of the initiation rite. There was a huge conflict between the traditionalists on the one hand, who placed great premium on the act of slicing the female genitalia as a rite of passage into womanhood and on the other, the reformists who wanted the tradition to be abolished for its social and health consequences. I became the poster child of the debate. The reformists won the day. I was taken to the school against my parents' wishes. As a result, the traditionalist called me offensive names like *gborka* – a disapproving reference to a female or male who has not been initiated into any of the secret societies (Bondo

15

for women, or Poro for men).

I was taunted in every corner. Sometimes they had set *traps* for me in public places to fulfill their dream of initiating me into the Bondo society. I became the town's most wanted *Gborka*. Luckily, for so it seemed at the time, I enjoyed the protection of the reformists, who perceived me as a trophy saved from the treacherous hands of the traditionalists. Nevertheless, I suffered humiliation from my peers. Even on my graduation day, I could still hear the scornful name of *Gborka*, louder than the sparking engines of the departing vehicles leaving the college premises. It was that condemnation and slurs that had eventually driven me from the village of my birth. I had become absorbed in my pursuit of western education.

During vacations, I had dreaded going to the village because of the animosity my friends had born against me. I was different in the way I had dressed, talked, and behaved. The western style education had rubbed off on me, creating an individual that had become an object of jealousy, envy, and sometimes ridicule.
There seemed to be a proportional relationship between my academic achievement and my alienation. The degree certificate I was now holding was not only a certificate of academic achievement, but also a certificate of isolation. It was equivalent to the number of teachers, lecturers and businessmen I had gone to bed with to acquire it. It was also equivalent to the years of detachment and years of sojourn in a make- believe world.
"Is it worth the price?"
This was my dilemma; perhaps it was my feminine weakness which was getting the better of me. Whatever it is, I did not

know… I burst into tears and wept furiously.

When I regained my self-control, I found the compound plunged into darkness. It was certain that there had been a power outage. I wiped my tears and I took a firm grip of myself and my certificate and moved towards the bus station vowing never to cry again. The feel of the certificate in my hands gave me the false belief that it would earn me a place in the universe. I went to the bus station only to find it deserted. I decided to remove the gown so that no one would recognise me as one of those that earlier graduated from the university. I waited, hoping that I would get a lift. After waiting for a while, I glanced at my Cartier wrist watch; I was surprised to learn that it is almost midnight. I folded my academic gown, removed my long heeled shoes and started to descend Tower hill on which the college was situated. I left, knowing I was leaving the University for the Universe, armed with a certificate smeared with question marks. *Is this the price?*

I got to Lower Faculty flats with a finality pronounced by the thudding of my feet on the street. I remembered how many times I have trekked this road to fend for resources to maintain my needs and make-believe status in college. Everyone and everything was fair game. I needed money, clothes and other accessories that gave the impression of achievement. We smeared dirt on ourselves in order to look good. Yet we used the dirt acquired status to measure our humanity. I slept with different kinds of men and thought for a while that I was of equal status to the men I slept with. I walked tall with the dirty status that robbed off on me for associating with them, a status I had acquired by breaching the laws of decency. Together with these dirty

17

politicians and dirty businessmen, we had created a society in which dirt had become the standard of measurement. The politicians had given us a little of their dirt in the form of material things and influence in order to increase our status among colleagues on campus. We created a world where dirt was the social currency with which we measured our social capital. The dirty syndrome took many forms. Sometimes we created artificial scarcity of essential goods by hoarding them. We measured our status by sourcing them, using our chain of dirty connections. The dirtiest victim was usually at the helm – the president, and then we became little presidents by association.

Things would have been a whole lot different if I had listened to Aminata, my roommate. Unlike most of us on campus she knew what she wanted. She seemed to have an internalised value system that was dirt proof. One night I returned to our grave-like bedroom in the University Hall of residence and found Aminata at her study table, as always. Everything in the room was mine: the cooker, the television, the fridge, and more. My belongings invaded her space except for a quarter of the room which I left for her to put her jeans, tee shirts and trainers. As for provisions, she merely stocked garri sugar and milk like the hard-up boys of Donovan Hall. I had just been appointed president of *Zoo* Club, and I was extremely happy. However, Aminata was not impressed for something that is for all reckoning, the highest social status on college.

The appointment was recognition of the status I had earned myself. I now belonged to the high and mighty of Sumbuya University. Guys of all clans and ages sucked up to me to enhance their prospects of being invited to our end-of-the-year party, a major social calendar and a parading of 'who was who' on campus. The club's chairlady status would take me beyond the borders of the university. Was my roommate impressed by the accolade? No, she wasn't. .

"Zainab I think this club thing will distract you further from your studies. Yes, it will increase your scope of social interaction, but it will not go down well for you."

I went into a defensive mood, protecting my ego.

"Are you jealous because you have not been invited? You always talk as if you are better than others."

"Oh, my God!" exclaimed Aminata. "What put that thought in your mind? I am only trying to give you an alternative opinion.

"Keep your opinion to yourself. I am now a *Zoo* babe."

"So what?" retorted Aminata.

She was a peaceful room mate who hardly quarrelled and talked in a subdued voice, laden with logic. For some illogical reason, I was just fired up, too animated.

"So what?" I queried.

"Can't you see the differences in my wardrobe?"

I took off on a Vanity Fair trip with my concord-like ego. Aminata called out to me, like a hostile control tower, before my plane could gather full throttle and my fuselage start puffing smoke, "Have you ever stopped to ask the price of these things? I don't mean the Leones you pay. I mean the real cost. For example, this antiquated piece of television. How much did you pay for it? Let's say a hundred Leones. That's the cost of the history book you kept borrowing down block. The real cost is what you did (and to whom) in order to get it."

I went cold, like a mummified corpse. The real price of the

19

things in my room began to pop up. The generator cost several nights with a custom officer. The blouse I was wearing cost one night in the company of a faceless businessman. All of a sudden, everything in the room took a life of its own, creating grim shadows in my colorful life. Faces of men, bedrooms of cheap hotels, and obscene acts popped up everywhere in the room, losing their physicality and melting into a giant interrogative. The broken Toyota car cost a lot. The real price I had paid for all the material things I was feeling proud about suddenly became unbearable like the weight of an albatross on the ancient Mariner's neck.

I burst into tears, hoping that the tears would cleanse my afflicted soul and wipe out the gray area that had eclipsed the colour in my life. Aminata came closer and held me tight to her bosom like a mother would do to a distressed child. "Sorry Zee I did not mean to hurt you."
"No, Aminata. I should be sorry for my outburst. I started it. I wish you had told me or thought aloud about this before it was too late. I have made a mess of myself."
"No, you have not. You can still make it right."
I surveyed the room again. My eyes caught a piece of old blouse on the floor which we now use as a duster for cleaning our room.

The memory of my undoing returned again with unparalleled force. This time I could feel the weight of the fat minister on my chest, the staccato rhythm of his strained breath as he tried to reaffirm to me what remained of his manhood. The strong stench of his nicotine stained breath diluted with odor of vodka, still pervaded my nostrils. I could still hear his groans of ecstasy as he thrust himself inside me. What did I get in return? The blouse which has now turned into a rag!

Did the same fate await my being? The answers to these questions were beyond me, or rather, I was too scared to contemplate them. What I had given up to be counted in the 'Vanity Fair' could never be replaced. What I had received was now torn and tattered, and the connection was glaring: I had exchanged my essence not for love, but for ephemeral possessions.

Aminata was right. The price was not the financial cost; it was not even the alternative. The real price was what I gave to get the money. I gave myself up; the part of me that has no honour. That part of me paid for that rag on the floor and those 'rags' in the wardrobe. As a matter of fact, I had an identity pact with that rag, thus making me a rag.

"At what price?" was the question that unleashed another floodgate of thoughts? I wish I had this quarrel with Aminata long ago. I wished Aminata had talked to me long ago; I mean, talked to me in a manner as graphic as she had just done. I tried to undress in order to slip into something comfortable. As I placed my wristwatch on the table, my mind reeled back to the same question: "What is the price?" Like a time machine, the watch transported me back in time, breaking down the psychic walls I had created to block out that aspect of my life. It was one of the ministers, I know because I did not go to bed with any one in that month of May.

With the exams fever on, we had formed study groups. Selecting a study group was an art form; first, you had to make a list of the smart guys in class. Choose your entry point. Most of the time, you had to flirt with one of the guys and give him the impression that you might one day date him, either openly or covertly in what was called in college parlance, 'underground' - UG for short. Your guy of choice needed to have possessed strong leadership qualities: smart, fluent and capable of protecting you from the radical guys who thought all *Zoo* Girls were phonies. In most cases, these UG relationships had ended up becoming college boyfriend or girlfriend.

The other factor was finances: you must have been financially capable in order to meet most of the cost of the study groups, such as the purchase of candles, kerosene, coffee, food and kola nuts. It would have made economic sense to belong to groups with two benefactors; this reduced the burden on one person. During our Qualifying year (the third year at university), I joined a perfect study group. I avoided going to town. My life was a routine, bordering on ritual.

One day I was coming from the library when I met Sandra by *Bus Tik*.
"*Girls*, I have been trying to reach you. I got something for you," Sandra said excitingly.
She always brought goods to sell on campus from her mum's boutique in town. I happened to have been one of her best customers. Sandra was a smart salesgirl. She knew our weakness, and she harped at them with maximum result. She knew we were vain and strove to out-dress each other. Sandra exhibited her goods to a group of girls with like taste and disposition and got them droll over the items before proclaiming to all: "They are not for sale. They

22

belong to Zainab, a special order."

The news of a special order made the rounds in the grapevine of fashion. By the time Sandra had got to you with your special order, all your rational economic judgment would have dissipated. You remained emotive. It was your emotion that made the decision to buy. Refusing to pay for a special order sent the wrong signals among friends and other opposing camps. Rumors of the status of your relationship with your 'boy jackass' - the uncomplimentary status given to men mostly dated for their financial status - will make rounds in a manner that could be harmful to you. In some cases, other opposing groups may want to attempt to snatch him from you, and in the process, spill vital information about your covert social operations. Sandra knew this and utilised the information to her advantage. Her sales strategy was a mix of subtle blackmail and wit. If ever you tried to rationalise the purchase based on your financial status or other factors, Sandra would come in with her sales pitch!

"Zainab, if you don't need it I will pass it on to Daphne", she would say.

She made sure she called a rival group. This was how our wardrobes got packed with things we didn't need.

The day Sandra brought this Cartier wrist watch and matching chain, she needed not to use her last trade pitch of suggesting an alternative buyer. I was interested the moment she showed them to me. That weekend, I abandoned my studies and dashed to town to get the money from my minister 'sugar daddy' - an older and more successful male lover. I got the money plus an unwanted pregnancy, as a direct product of unprotected sex. The other extras like sexually transmitted diseases, I did not bother to contemplate.

I missed my menstrual period that May month. I had to tag along until the end of the exams in June. I went to see my minister friend to tell him about my situation. He was in his office, shuffling papers, perhaps to give me the impression that he was working hard.

"I am pregnant," I announced.

He dropped the papers on the table, removed his reading lenses, and gazed at me squarely.

"What did you just say?" he interrogated.

"You heard me the first time. I am pregnant."

"And who is responsible?" he asked.

I looked at him with seething rage and contempt.

"I will not be here if it was not you. What do you take me for, a prostitute?"

I deliberately uttered the last word a decibel higher than the others for maximum dramatic effect. The purpose was to give him a hint of my intention to take the issue to the public domain. He noticed the hint and walked towards me, more subdued. He put his arm around me and said, "Calm down."

"I won't calm down!" I shrugged away from him.

"Zainab, you know I am a respected married man? You see, this will ruin my reputation and marriage."

I eyed him again with more contempt. "And it won't ruin my reputation? So you think I don't have anything to lose because I am not a minister? When you were drooling on top of me, you did not think of your family and reputation."

He saw my drift and became subdued.

"I am sorry you are getting me all wrong. What do we do?"

Eventually, we reached a decision to abort.

24

A few days later, I sprawled out in a theatre with my legs fettered and numbed by anesthetics. I almost died in the process. The doctor later told me that my chances of having another child were very limited. All of this was for a Cartier watch and chain that I later learned was a pitiful imitation of the real product. For that I gave my blood, my honor, and my unborn child. Yet, this close to death experience did not give me a wakeup call. I still kept chasing phantoms of reality until the night Aminata raised the question: "what is the price?"

Since that night I had been wallowing on a journey of self-discovery on a path strewn with regrets and unborn children. The question took away the joy of being elected as the chairlady of the *Zoo* Club, a designation that meant being at the pinnacle of the college's social stratification structure. Now, it has a ring of hollowness about it because of four words pieced together and delivered at the right moment, with the right tone and mood. I cried myself to sleep with a resolve to transform my life.

The following morning, I tendered my resignation as a chairlady and member of *Zoo* Club. My resignation was like an earthquake in social circles. The nature and texture of my friends began to change. Most of my social friends who had associated with me because of my membership in the *Zoo* club avoided me. Some were even downright hostile. The situation got worse when I donated all the material things acquired during my days as a glamour girl. Unlike other members of Zoo Club whose intention was genuine social interaction, mine was to acquire a false status and to use it to manipulate men to my advantage. Aminata`s intervention on that night exposed my inner-self and I didn't like what I saw from my psychological portrait. My resignation was a means of self-atonement. I dropped from the top three well-dressed girls in college to the un-rated category of grinning jeans and T-shirts. Ironically, I felt well dressed in my pair of jeans and T-shirt than I had with those glamorous outfits. Simply put, I didn't have to go naked to buy them. I became like Aminata and those other girls who took pride in being who they were, girls from poor backgrounds striving to be the first to acquire education in their families.

I started seeing people for who they were not what they wore or how they smelled. I celebrated life for what it was, stripped of all material things. Aminata became my mentor; her philosophy of life became my philosophy. We were like conjoined twins. Being a true friend to her enabled me to appreciate the true meaning of friendship. We shared the little we had and didn't have to smear ourselves with dirt to belong. The difference in me after that night of my argument with Aminata saved in my mind's filing system. I called it the night of too many questions. Whenever I found myself defaulting to the old habits, I just opened my file and clicked to the night of the interrogative. The contents glared and blared in my mind's screen. That night was stored in my mainframe - the mind - with the subconscious acting as a backup.

I know now that I didn't need to lease part of me or the whole of me to a club to have an identity. I believed in myself.

One day I was in the room alone reading, and my mind

surfed back to my past life, a life in which dirt was the yardstick with which to measure status in society. The dirt came in various forms: dirty money stolen from state vaults or influence emitting from the backsides of dirty politicians who managed the national assets for self-gratification. I wished Aminata had talked to me earlier, or I wish I had listened more. I would not have got myself mixed up. At that moment it occurred to me that there were others like me who didn't have the opportunity of a "night of interrogatives" with Aminata. I thought we must reach out to others in the manner that Aminata had reached out to me. We could have been saving the soul of a nation.

I was deep in thought when I heard the clanking of Aminata's keys at the door, returning me to the real world.
"Girls, are you shooting for a division one? I can see you are oozing with knowledge; the temperature of the room is academically at a melting point", Aminata teased.
"You will be surprised to know that my mind is miles away from reading," I replied.
"Where has it gone to?" enquired Aminata.
"I have been thinking of the night you talked to me, the night of the interrogative? The night you asked me the question: …
"At what price?" Aminata butted in.
"Of course, I remember, but why do you keep going back to that night?"
I paused before responding.
"Because that night changed my life, and I have been wondering if we could package that experience into a movement to help save the likes of many who are lost in the glittering glamour and have forgotten the essence of their being".

27

Aminata interrupted. "But the studies and…
I cut in again, saying, "We can make a difference".
The discussion evolved, and by the end of the evening we decided to form a movement that focused on dealing with intimate friends. Our strategy was simple: talk to our friends in private with the sole aim of restoring their sense of security. Let the friend know she is a whole person, a person held in high esteem and that she didn't have to go to the extremes of trading herself to buy rags.

There was sincerity in our dealings with our colleagues and a marked standard of privacy in the mode and manner of the message. A few weeks after launching our campaign, we began to observe changes on campus. A wave of reality swept through the campus, particularly among our target group. The dress code on campus started to change from Vanity Fair costumes to jeans, T-shirts, and African costumes. Some of the T-shirts carried prints pronouncing personal philosophies, like: "I am not dirt" and "You look good at what price?"

Apart from the T-shirt and stickers, the compound engaged in debates revolving on the new phenomenon. The consciousness spread beyond costumes; it invaded the classrooms. Students increased their participation in classroom discussions. The notion of sucking up to lecturers to woo their sympathy simmered down. The absence of a secretariat and a structure for our movement was baffling to many observers. We let the message speak, not the messenger.

However, our drive which raised the consciousness of some female students did not go down well in some quarters.

The aspect of our theory of dirt as a yardstick to measure our humanity seemed to be disturbing to many observers. The rendition and appreciation of the campaign varied from person to person and circumstance to circumstance. The philosophy, if we could call it that, was couched in slang in Krio, one of the country's national languages: "I nor mix pan dorty game" meaning "I am not a party of the dirty game." The slang somehow found its way on the tongues of lecturers and non-teaching staff.

Some junior staff discussed it as a student slang that will perish in linguistic dustbin like all other slangs. Others treated it much more seriously, for they interpreted it to mean the commencement of a student revolt. The fact that the female students were undergoing a change in attitude was baffling. Some lecturers and students, who gathered information on so called subversive activities, got a field day reporting the new trend to the university court for onward transmission to the national ruling party office in town.

The court was structured and staffed to protect the party against real and imagined enemies. It was through this system that a group of students were dismissed from college for making "careless talk" - uncomplimentary remarks against the political system. Students who reported on activities of their colleagues were also on government's payroll. Then, the ruling government was absolutely paranoid. The paranoia set in after a series of student strikes that nearly crippled the state. The Government's reaction to the students' unrest led to the disenfranchisement of the people, through a single party system. This meant that there were no longer legitimate channels for people to vent out their grievances. All other democratic institutions were cast in the big show of the single party. The only dissenting

29

voice was the university. The dissent started as slang, which changed to slogans and the slogans became a movement. The movement translated to a match from the university campus into the city. This was how the 'No College Strike' almost brought about the downfall of the ruling party at the time.

It did not come as a surprise to see the party machinery on college stepping up their activities against our campaign against *dirt*. However, the nature of our operation made it difficult for them to pin it on anyone. There was no office, no paper work, nothing, because the whole movement was an idea dropped into one's mind. Like most oppressive regimes, the main idea of the ruling party at the time was to control every aspect of people's lives. They tried to control what the citizens thought, who they interacted with, and how they passed their time. It got worse, for the system grew more paranoid. The slang took on a life of its own; it travelled via thoughts and tongues through the many cannels or short cut routes to the city. It landed on the tongues of the city guys who stripped it of its academic background and took ownership of the movement. They composed songs which were calculated to hurt the ego of the ministers and their functionaries.
"Ah mba na dorti", meaning "It is dirt".

The public turned the idea of dirt into an abusive language against the politicians. Very few people knew what the meaning was; they just delivered different forms of it to a point that the ruling class became worried.

This is how it all started.

The surveillance and the harassment began. At this point, a radical journalist who was hated by the system for his uncomplimentary stand wrote an article tracing the origin of the slang and its meaning. The article was spiteful and full of examples of dirt in the system. The article concluded with a poem:

> dirt everywhere in the head of the head
> dirt everywhere in the treasure of our treasury
> stinking dirt, rife with stench

One day the presidential motorcade was passing along the slum-like markets of Doves' Cut when the petty traders started shouting the slang:
"Ah mba nar dorti".
The taunting gathered momentum. The crowd of singers increased, and they barricaded the road, putting the presidential entourage under siege. Pa Baimba, the commissioner of police, had to release his special forces with orders to shoot and kill. The incident spread to other parts of the city, and soldiers were called in to put out the riot. By the time the crises simmered down, ten corpses lay in the street.

The president conveyed a meeting and a rather brutal investigation began. By then, it did not occur to me that there was any connection between the advice Aminata had given to me and the riot. On the night of the riot there was power outage, which meant that we had to study with lantern and candles; I had to go to the study hall with my lantern to join my study group. Aminata was already there with her group. The mood that evening was sombre. It was more like a vigil for the people killed in the riot. The number of people killed in the riot was difficult to assess. Accounts in the government controlled media claimed that ten people had died in accidental circumstances. Other independent sources indicated that the number was ten times bigger. Nearly everybody in the study hall was disturbed. The matter was made worse by the fact that the government declared a curfew, which meant we could not go to town and check on our families.

The torment in everyone's mind found expression in the study hall. The brutality of the government was widely discussed. The spin that they put on the radio, which made the sporadic incident look like a coup, baffled most listeners. I moved close to Aminata because I had noticed a solemn mood in her more than anyone else.

"Are you okay, dear?" I asked her.

Aminata looked at me straight in the eyes, and I noticed tears in her eyes.

"I am okay, I guess you can say that," she said in a rather staggering voice.

The whole study hall looked like a funeral parlour. Perhaps it is a funeral for a nation in the clutches of a dictator.

"We are all potential corpses waiting to be killed again and again, like we were killed yesterday", I muttered aloud the lines of a poem I read in the press.

It was a bombshell, the muttering stopped, and everyone turned to me in the hope that there was more where that came from.

The student body was looking for leadership. I was taken aback by the impact of those lines on the students. It dawned on me that the whole riot started with words pieced together to form a sentence and each sentence put together to form an idea. The same words and idea spilled over to the city, triggered a riot, a riot that has led to the deaths of many people.

Words are not just words'; they are balm that soothes the soul, bombs that fire the spirit. Words are weapons, land mines. Words are not just words. The moment was not right for any political utterance. There were student stooges who could rally anything said here to their puppet masters in town.

I picked up my bag and my lantern and signaled to Aminata to do the same.
"Yes, we are all potential corpses, mummified by fear to stand up for what we believe in. I was shocked first to hear Aminata's rendition of a poem displayed at Chukes Press and by the reaction of the student body to her poem. Students started banging at their tables, shouting slogans like: "Freedom to our people!" "Death to the traitors!"

Among the students at the Student Union building was a notorious party stooge known and hated by almost all. He noticed the mood of the students and ran for his life. The whole student body chased him, shouting: "Death to the traitor!" The campus went rowdy. Flashlights, candle lights, and lantern lights emerged at every corridor, creating shadows of shadows. This indeed was a night like no other.

The disturbance reached a crescendo when, in defiance of radio broadcast the student started singing the derogatory 'Dorti kolombo' song which sparked off the riot in town. I navigated through the furniture and crowd to grab Aminata's hand. "Let's return to our room; this is beginning to get out of hand," I said.

I literally dragged her from the madding crowd to our bedroom for a moment of reflection. Indeed Aminata was in a reflective mood all through the journey to the room. She found space on her overcrowded table for the pile of books that she had brought from the student union hall. I dumped mine on my bed.

"I feel guilty. I started it" Aminata spoke in a sad tone.

"What did you think you started?" I inquired.

"The riot; the disturbance this evening," she said sadly.

I paused. "How could you have started a riot in town at the slums of Dove Cut when you were with us all through the day"? I queried again.

"I started it by my utterances. Don't you remember the slang that mutated to a slogan, and a song was born in this room by these lips during the night of the interrogative?"

My mind switched to the introductory lesson of our philosophy class: 'The theory of causation.' If you are thinking along the lines of 'cause and effect' then, don't blame yourself, because I started it through my phoney life style and vain existence. If I were a sober person, you would have had no reason to utter that speech during the night of the interrogatives; the 'dirt theory' would still be dangling in the graveyard of unborn concepts. I burst into tears as the full gravity of how my life could affect the world around us dawned on me.

Aminata noticed that I had hijacked the guilt that was exclusively hers. "Zainab, this society was rotten to the core before you came along. What I said about dirt was not an image of the moment. It was not a time-bound comment. It had a historical baggage beyond the thought that

34

preceded those words. And the thoughts beyond those words will survive you. You should not feel guilty about...."

She paused.

"I thought I heard a gunshot."

I thought so too, but I dismissed it on the pretext that it could be the Special Forces maintaining order in town. By the time I had delivered the last syllable of my denial, I heard a rather loud gun shot with fragments of whatever was fired clattering on our roof.

The sporadic gunshots followed by the cacophony of cries unleashed unprecedented chaos on the campus. From our corridor, I could see the flash of fire from the Kalashnikov guns fired by the invaders. The stories of Party thugs invading the compound to stop strikes were many and rendered differently to successive generations of students. The spin made by the thugs who were now highly placed, diluted the facts and almost buried the facts to the archives. The invasion that we witnessed that night enabled these facts to resurface. We were now the eye witnesses to the massacre of students by a coercive government. The thugs were in our mist and everyone went into panic mode. Female students changed into jeans to create obstacle to would be rapists, rushed into the dark corridor, banging doors to alert fellow students about the attack. After banging on a few doors, it occurred to me that the shots and the cries were drowning my voice.

I retraced my steps back to my room without any purpose in mind. I crossed students running randomly in the hallway. Some were carrying their valuables, others carried just irrelevant items. On my way, I heard a scream from one

35

room. I paused to check; someone was locked out. I told her to get off the door, and I rammed it with all my strength. The century- old door flunked open.
"Try and evacuate your room. These thugs are in the hostels already!" I snarled at her.

I could hear the screams and smelled the odor of cheap rum in the dark corridor on my way to my room. I almost gave up the effort of moving against the human tide when I thought I heard Aminata's voice. I mustered all my strength to bulldoze my way against the human traffic. As I moved, I felt the irritating feel of tear gas in the air.

All of a sudden, I started moving at speed, for it seemed as if the student body had conspired to transport me to my room to answer the call of my friend. From the darkness, someone shouted, "Jump from your corridor the thugs have blocked the entrance to the building!"

The shout gave an explanation as to why I was moving faster than I wished to. The human tide was sailing in my direction. I burst into the room in commando style to find the thug ripping Aminata's pants. The head in his pants had taken control over him; he was on fire. He did not see me coming. I grabbed the lantern, and swung it with all the rage inside me. I hit him on the head, the kerosene splash on him, setting him on fire to quench the fire in his pants. I grabbed the nylon mosquito net and wrapped it on him. He screamed like a wounded lion. In his attempt to quench the fire, he jumped into the other net on the opposite bed.

The second mosquito net also caught fire and engulfed him at the same time. The smell of his roasted skin took over the room. The blazing fire and his cry of agony gave a picture of a pagan ritual. We dashed in the direction of the corridor. As we were scaling the height before jumping, I saw him coming to us in flames, a gun in his hand. "Jump! He has a gun!"

I landed wrongly and sprained my ankle. I turned to look for Aminata. I saw her silhouette on the floor, dead from gunshot wounds. I grabbed her, trying to resuscitate her, but it was too late: Aminata was dead, killed by that thug who was burning in hell even before he was dead.

Aminata, the epitome of excellence, a symbol of decency, was killed by the dirtiest man of them all. I feel a part of me was gone forever; there was no longer any purpose in existence. My survival mode that was pumping adrenalin since the thugs entered the compound not only stopped, it went into reverse. My whole self -retired into a shell of reticence. I could no longer hear the gunshots, neither could I see the chaos around me, nor feel or perceive the danger. Aminata was dead; it was like Zainab was dead too.

In the abyss of my grief and guilt, I became consumed by bitterness in a manner I had never before imagined. I wanted to hurt that burning barbeque of a man more than ever; I wanted to hurt those dictators who schemed against their people; I wanted to hurt them just as they had hurt me; I wanted to hurt them as they had hurt Aminata. I stood up by the remains of Aminata, watching the thug burn to ashes.

I lifted the remains of Aminata and staggered towards the Lower Faculty. The sight of Aminata's corpse emboldened the students. They stopped running and confronted the thugs. The thugs were also weakened by the fact that their leader had been burned alive. They started running for their lives. They ran with their tails between their legs, chased by the emboldened students.

We kept vigil throughout the night, taking turns in tending to the injured. Throughout the night, the government spewed propaganda to cover up the act of the thugs. In the morning, I took Aminata's body and led the demonstration to the seat of government – the house of parliament. The solemnity of the demonstration converted the country into grief of such magnitude that baffled the government. By the time the demonstration terminated at the home of Aminata, the government had issued a disclaimer denying any involvement with the thugs who attacked the students.

As I strolled down the hill, clutching my certificate, I recalled that painful match down this very hill, carrying the corpse of Aminata. I recalled the many times I had gone down this hill to become a glamour girl. I recalled the many trips that wreaked havoc on my life to the extent that I needed Aminata to talk sense into me during the night of the interrogative.

This descent from Sumbuya College was like a descent to the grave of Aminata. The pebbles on my bare feet were like the pebbles we threw back on Aminata in the 'ashes-to-ashes' ritual. I was like an ash burned out long in that graveyard. I am now descending to conjoin with the ashes left behind by Aminata. I resolve to be the ash that will not go down without a fight. I owe it to Aminata who should not have died in vain.

In my depressed mood, I had found a glowing zone that brought life to my soul. It was the satisfaction of knowing that I roasted the man who killed my friend.

Armed with my certificate, my mind reeled back to the question: "Is this the price?"

Alimamy Rassin Kamara

A STRANGE KIND OF VACATION

After travelling for over 200 miles, Bampya alighted at the door steps of his half sister and brother-in-law in the village of Zapa. Amie, his sister, and Karim, his brother-in-law, were very pleased to have him with them. Amie took her brother into a room which she told him would be his while he stayed on vacation.

It was a very spacious room with a large comfortable bed. There was a wardrobe and shoe rack at the far end of the well lit room. Bampya was very pleased with himself, especially because in his village he sleeps on a mat placed on the floor for that purpose. He was feeling the cushion of the bed underneath the white sheets when Amie threw a towel to him.

"Go and have your bath and have your supper later."

Bampya obeyed dutifully.

It was a very brief bath, and he was soon having his supper. Bampya had to pause between mouthfuls to answer questions from his sister and brother-in-law about other family members and improvements in the village in general. He narrated all the events that happened in the village during the past year. He also told them the sad events, such as that of Kumrabai's tragic death.

Kumrabai had a very good job in the city. He had his family house in the village rebuilt and roofed with corrugated iron sheets. He also furnished it well to the envy of all in the

40

village. Kumrabai was the pride of the village and a model for all the children going to school at Macrogba and the neighboring villages.

One night, Kumrabai turned up at the village in a red Vauxhall car, which he told his father, Pa Fallah, that his company had given to him for his official use. Both old and young came round to stare at the car and to marvel at their kinsman's fortune. He took in his parents and a few friends and drove to the nearest headquarter town and back. Kumrabai, who was always immaculate, had been the talk of the village and become the ladies' man. He was loved and admired by many for his pleasant manners. For some strange reason, Kumrabai decided he needed protection against witchcraft, juju, and immunisation against bullets. The skills of the renowned Alpha Gbessay were sought. He came to the village as soon as he got the message of Pa Fallah. The assignment was carefully explained to him by Kumrabai himself. After listening carefully, Alpha Gbessay consulted his oracle. He used three horns tied at the bottom with red pieces of cloth for that purpose. After saying a few incantations, he pronounced that he could do the job, but Kumrabai had to provide him with a billy goat, a bottle of red wine, seven cola-nuts, a small bottle of cologne, and a big pot that Kumrabai could get into. He charged a fee of twenty thousand Leones; Kumrabai gave him an advance payment of ten thousand Leones.

Kumrabai promptly bought the required items for the job and it was decided that the immunisation job should start at nightfall. Alpha Gbessay then went into the bush and plucked various leaves for his trade to ensure that he gave his new client the best. He then set the big pot on fire. He put all the herbs he had plucked into the pot along with ten gallons of water and left the contents to boil. He asked for a cube of black crude soap. He added some other ingredients which he hid from every onlooker's eyes. Finally, he put a bullet into the pot. Everything in the pot was *cooked* as the water boiled. He then summoned Kumrabai to join him and his assistants in a shrine that had been hurriedly constructed. As Kumrabai entered the shrine, Alpha Gbessay told him he was going to confiscate every piece of his clothing since the client never wore any clothes in a shrine of that nature. So Kumrabai took off shoes, trousers, and shirt. Even his briefs and his gold plated watch were confiscated. What a greedy *Marabou*!

Now, Kumrabai was in the nude and sitting on a mat with Alpha Gbessay, who took out a bottle of foul smelling oil and applied it liberally all over his client's body. When he was satisfied, he instructed Kumrabai to get into the pot. Kumrabai stared at him in disbelief. Alpha Gbessay ordered him to step into the pot just as he himself dipped his hand into the boiling contents. Kumrabai then tried the water with his hand and was amazed that the boiling water was not hot! He then climbed into the pot and sat in as he had been instructed. Alpha Gbessay scooped some water and herbs and washed Kumrabai from head to toe. When he was satisfied Kumrabai was clean, he asked him to step out of the pot and sit on a stool at the corner of the shrine. He sat there until the water on his body had evaporated. Satisfied, Alpha Gbessay loaded a gun with a live bullet and asked Kumrabai to stand up and face him. Kumrabai got up, walked to the middle of the shrine, and waited. Alpha Gbessay aimed the gun at Kumrabai's chest and then pulled the trigger. A loud noise broke the silence of the night as the bullet tore into Kumrabai's chest, ripping both his heart and lungs. There was a splutter of blood. It oozed from his chest and mouth. Slowly, he fell at Alpha Gbessay's feet. Panic stricken, Alpha Gbessay said, "Oh, somebody must have undone me. Oh, my God! I have killed somebody, and now the law is going to get me. Oh, God! What am I to do now?" he sobbed.

Pa Fallah who had been watching it all could not believe that his son had suddenly turned into a corpse. He fell on his son and wept over him. They did not even realise that the sound of the gun had attracted the other villagers who came to see what was going on. They all started to weep aloud when they saw what had happened. The village chief then sent two of his messengers to go and make a report at the nearest police station. Alpha Gbessay was subsequently arrested. That was the end of the onetime hero of Macrogba. Amie and her husband felt bad about the tragedy that had struck the village, and the tragic manner in which Kumrabai had departed this world.

Bampya also told his sister about his examination results. He was ranked first in a class of 35 pupils again. Amie was always proud of her brother and boasted about his academic prowess. After answering many questions from both his listeners, Bampya was allowed to go to bed and get himself a well-earned sleep.

Vacationing at Amie's had always been exciting. Apart from the fun Bampya had mixing with kids of other schools, he also enjoyed the exploits of illicit miners in the village. Their lives were daily encounters with the police who prevented them from mining diamonds. They were always chased away, but it seemed the more they were chased out, the more they schemed to outwit and beat the Mine Wardens and police. It was during this vacation that Bampya saw and touched a diamond for the first time. You can imagine the smile on Bampya's face when Amie called him into her room and placed on the bed about seven brilliant stones of very high value. Amie told her brother the approximate value of each gem in the local market.

Bampya was invited one evening to attend a new club's meeting at the marketplace. He was reluctant to go because he did not have any decent clothes to wear like the other kids vacationing with him. After much persuasion by his closest friend in the village, Bampya eventually attended with Komba. At the meeting there were students from various secondary schools in the country. Bampya was thought of as from a humble background as evidenced by his thread-bare shirt and trousers. The other fellows whose parents were well-off displayed their immaculate clothes and smart turnout. They were very boisterous and flippant in their speech, and this behaviour made Bampya very subdued and uneasy. Some of the boys were already on familiar terms with some of the girls. So you can only imagine Bampya's relief when a sixth former, who acted as chairman, rapped the table to get the attention of the meeting. He gave a preamble of what the club is supposed to do for the mutual benefit of the villagers and the members. After his introduction, he invited suggestions from the rest of the club. Everybody wanted to speak at once. The boys, it seemed were out to impress the girls, who were very passive during this uproar. The English spoken by those well-dressed boys was so poor that Her Majesty, the Queen of England, could not have resisted

44

ordering their execution. The girls only giggled as their 'paramours exhibited their ignorance and rank inadequacies.'

Indeed, it is true, the word of caution: "He who knows not and knows not that he knows not - shun him. He is a fool."

Most of those fellows were fools in their attempts or pretences to speak impeccable English. Bampya wondered what the girls felt about the boys' shameless display. I am not suggesting here that one must not try speaking what one learns. It is pretending to know something you know nothing about that I find irritating.

After they had had their laughter, Komba asked Bampya to help the situation. Bampya declined at first, but as Komba insisted on his contribution to the meeting, Bampya showed his right hand, indicating that he wanted to speak. The rest of the folks at the meeting laughed as Bampya got up in his old clothes. He was undaunted and waited patiently for the laughter to fizzle out. When it was quiet to his satisfaction, Bampya made his contribution so brilliant and impeccable that all the girls applauded his oratory, and the boys could not help joining in the applause. Komba proudly shook his hand as he sat down. That speech was the turning point to Bampya's popularity. At election time, everybody wanted Bampya to become president, secretary, and social secretary, all of which he humbly declined. The acting chairman could not take it any longer. So, he asked Bampya to explain why he was declining all the nominations for the various honorary positions. Bampya simply told him and the rest of the members that he did not want to commit himself. After the election of officers, the new president decided that members should work toward a *Back-to-school* dance.

A girl by the name of Adama volunteered to pay for Bampya, and she did that at once to the admiration of the other boys and the annoyance of her boyfriend, Foday. At the end of the meeting, both boys and girls milled around Bampya, congratulating him for his outstanding contribution. Many questions were asked, among which were: What school do you attend? What form are you?

Games of football were also organised to raise funds for the dance. Again Bampya was the most outstanding. He scored the first and winning goals in their 3: 2 victory over another mining village. He now had many fans, both male and female. Adama even volunteered to buy a pair of trousers, shirt and shoes for Bampya so that he could attend the dance. Bampya promptly declined the offer. He did not want to spoil his new friendship with Foday, Adama's boyfriend. Amie had a new set of clothes made for her brother for the dance, which had been the talk of the town.

At the dance, almost everybody was there. More people turned up to celebrate the victory of the football match, while others went to see which girls they might catch for the night and there were many to choose from/. Meanwhile Bampya was being pampered by Adama and her friends. She bought soft drinks and snacks for her new friend. Gradually a crowd gathered around Bampya, each man congratulating him for a great game and offering him a drink which he politely turned down. Being a shy guy, Bampya decided he had had enough for the evening, excused himself and left for home. He was almost there when he heard someone call: "Bampya, please wait for me!"

Bampya stopped and turned around. Adama came to him, panting. "Why did you leave us so soon?" She demanded.

"I have never been out so late before. Besides, I don't want to annoy my sister by waking her up while opening my room door," Bampya replied.

"Let's go to your room, Bampya," Adama suggested.

"What are we going to my room for? Let's talk here," Bampya replied.

I don't want anybody to see us, but there's something I want to tell you." Adama said. Bampya then led the way to his room.

Since there was no chair in the room, they both sat on the bed. "What is it that you want to tell me?" Bampya asked.

"It's about Foday, my boyfriend," She now looked Bampya in the eyes. "He is jealous of you and is afraid that he will lose me to you."

"Oh yes? When did I become an object of jealousy? Why would you want to bother yourself with a poor thing like me?" Bampya asked.

"Listen, Bampya, I love you so much - much more than my parents. I am a proud girl as you already know and have never told a boy that I love him. Boys come to me and tell me how much they care for me, and I treat them like dirt, but you are irresistible. Please Bampya, say you love me. Please go on and say it. I will go and drown if you say no. Go on, now! Say you love me; please say it!"

Bampya was moved by the girl's appeals and said the words that Adama wanted to hear. Adama smiled and kissed Bampya, who was not ready for that but found himself melting away. "Have you been in love before?" Adama asked.

"No," Bampya replied.

"Lucky me, virgin boy! Let's make love now. I will give you a watch tomorrow for taking your virginity."

"No, Adama. There's time for love. No, I cannot do it. I am very sorry to disappoint you, but that's how it is with me. No sex before marriage. I have a dream for the future to attain my goal in life; I must stay clear of women. No, I cannot touch a woman until I am old enough to do so and until I am married to whosoever will be my wife. I do hope you understand that," Bampya concluded.

"I want to be your wife, if you will marry me," Adama declared.

"In which case you will have to wait for ten years, and even at that, there's no guarantee that I will still want to marry you," Bampya suggested.

"O.K., I accept. We can be friends while we wait to see what the future has for us. I love you all the same, and please don't love any other girl in this village. Please promise me!"

"Yes, I promise you, Adama."

Adama then took Bampya's fingers and kissed them. She even tried sucking them, but Bampya withdrew his hand.

"I am so tired after all this dancing. Can I sleep for just ten minutes and then you will see me off to my house. O.K.?" Adama asked.

By the time her friend wanted to protest, she was lying in bed and pretending to be asleep; Bampya was visibly shaken by Adama's obstinacy. *What would my sister say if she learnt that Adama slept in his room?* As far as Adama was concerned, it was his problem and not hers. Adama slept till the early hours of the morning, when she woke up and told Bampya she was now going home. Bampya, now relieved and anxious to rid himself of this menace, got up and opened the door, letting Adama out. As he was about to see her off, he caught sight of Amie, who was doing her ablution before the *Salat Subr* prayers. If Amie was annoyed, she did not show it at that time. She just stared at the girl to identify her.

Soon after her prayers, Amie came to Bampya's room wearing a grave expression on her face to ask about the strange visitor.

"Aren't you ashamed of yourself? I am so ashamed and disappointed in you! I thought you were innocent. How could you do such a thing to me?" Amie demanded.

"I am still innocent and had nothing to do with that girl. I didn't want her to sleep in my room, but she insisted. How could I be rude to a girl! There was nothing between us. It's up to you to believe me or not," Bampya said.

He had never lied to his sister, and she knew that her brother must have been under intense pressure to have allowed such discourtesy to have taken place in his sister's household. In a solemn voice Amie told Bampya that she was concerned because he meant a lot to her, since both of them were the only children that have survived their late mum.

"I love you, Bampya, and I want the best for you. Please stay away from girls. There's time for every purpose under the sun. Let your studies take precedence over all other matters. Please take great care. You are both a brother and father to me, even though I am older than you," she concluded and left, as Bampya covered his face in shame and wept over his weakness to throw Adama out of the room...

Mohamed Sheriff

FAMILY AFFAIR

We sat waiting: my daughter, my disabled husband and I. We sat waiting in agitation, for our enemy will be brought to us any moment now. God, the merciful has answered our prayers. It is the least we could ask God for: to bring us our enemy so he will be punished for the wrong he had done to us, a grievous wrong.

One night, nine months ago, a grenade exploded in our home, tore my nine-months old granddaughter into bits and pieces, left my husband paralyzed with a stroke and damaged part of our house. My granddaughter was the only child to our only daughter, born after nine years of marriage! She was born nine months after her husband abandoned her because he thought our daughter was barren. Since that night nine months ago, I have known no peace. We have known no peace, none of us in our family. We feel that the only solace that we can get is to bring those responsible for our pain and misery to justice. We want to taste the sweetness of revenge. Since the rebel-junta alliance was kicked out of power, people everywhere have been meting out jungle justice to the brutes. We too have been praying that God will give us a name, a face, and soul to pay back in kind for what we have suffered.

Early this morning, an emaciated young rebel, about 18, appeared in town with a dirty white handkerchief raised above his head. Angry town folks wasted no time in pouncing on him and beating him until he was helpless. He would have been beaten to death, but as someone put it: "he didn't have much to beat, only a bag of bones, too pitiful to kill."

Jebbeh, my daughter and I found him lying in the dust in the town centre, with knife wounds all over his body. By then, the crowd was wondering what to do with him next.

"Where are you from?" someone asked.

 He managed to raise himself on his elbows. His speech was barely audible. "We were routed at our base outside Tongo, two months ago. Then, we went our several ways into the bush. We had no supply of food and had to make do with whatever seemed edible in the bush. Two weeks ago, we heard the president's offer of amnesty and call to surrender. We wasted no time and arrived about ten days ago to settle just outside this town. But, we were afraid to surrender for fear of the wrath of the people. The others are planning to go back into the bush. But I'm hungry, sick, weak, and tired of fighting. This is why I came to surrender".

The crowd fired more questions at him.

"Where exactly were you hiding?" a face in the crowd asked.

"We're hiding in the houses damaged by grenades just outside the town."

"Your grenades, right? You're one of those who attacked this town, nine months ago?"

"Answer the question!"

"It's possible that this rebel was involved in that attack. He has just said that they had their base outside Tongo. We know that the rebels who attacked us came from that area."

"Speak, you dog! Have you lost your voice?"

51

"His silence means guilt, and it's written all over his face."
The young man who started the questioning was huge, over six feet. He grabbed the unfortunate rebel by what was left of his shirt and slapped him twice.
"Now, answer the question!"
"I was not alone, sir. I was only obeying orders. The man who led us is also hiding in one of the damaged houses."

My heart started pounding wildly against my ribs. Maybe our prayers have been answered. I forced my way forward to the centre of the crowd where the boy laid wiping blood from the corners of his mouth. I went down on my knees and forced him to sit up. "Look at me," I pleaded. "I am a partial widow because my fifty-five year old husband is in bed at home, a victim of a stroke he suffered as a result of that attack. Everyone knew him to be one of the strongest farmers in town even at his age. Now he is useless. We have to take him to and out of bed, put him in his chair, feed him, bathe him, and dress him. This should have been the work of a male child, but my only son was captured in Tongo two years ago and forced to become a rebel. The last we heard about him was that he had been killed. That is not all. In that attack on this town, my house was badly damaged. The worst outcome for me personally was that my granddaughter was blasted into chopped meat by a grenade. Since that day, I have been praying to God, asking him to put the culprit in my hands. If you don't tell me, I swear by the Creator of this world, I'll squeeze your throat with my bare hands until the last breath expires from your pitiful body."

"Mammy Nana, don't soil your hands. Leave this to us. He will lead us there, and we'll bring them to you. Get up!" The huge youth barked at the miserable wretch.

The rebel pleaded desperately. No one heard him. He was dragged out of town to point out the others in their hideouts.

By the time we returned home, someone had told my husband. We met him in a state of great agitation. We got him out on the veranda in his armchair. Now we all wait, tensely. By this time, people had started gathering in front of our house awaiting the common enemy. It was a strange coincidence that all of this was unfolding in my presence as the only dead in that attack on our town was my granddaughter, Makallay. Many people were injured as they fled the town and many houses partially or completely destroyed by grenades, but no one was killed, except Makallay. We were lucky to have heard gunshots some minutes before the rebels attacked our village. So, we all had time to escape, but panic stricken, Jebbeh grabbed a pillow with the baby's wrapper thinking it was little Makallay. She was a mile out of town when she realized her mistake! My husband returned to town to get the child against all efforts to dissuade him. We need not have feared for his life as far as the rebels were concerned. They had not come to stay. They had come for plunder. My husband entered Jebbeh's room and found the mangled body of little Makallay. That was when he had his stroke. When he did not return after a couple of hours, we sent some young men after him. They found him lying in a coma on Jebbeh's bed beside the shredded body of my granddaughter. Now, sitting in his arm chair watching the road, he looks more excited than he has ever been since his stroke.

Chief Sidik, the traditional leader of our town, arrives suddenly with eight chiefdom policemen. It is clear that he has come to dissuade us from taking any action on our own against the rebels. He ignores the seat I offer him and gets straight to the point.

"Already I have sent for reinforcement of my men with some regular policemen. But I doubt whether they'll be here before the rebels are brought to town. This is where you come in, Mammy Nana. The lives of those rebels are in your hands. It is going to be difficult for me to stop the mob meting out jungle justice on those unfortunate souls, but you, who have suffered the most from their crimes, can spare them, if you choose to do so. If you tell them that you want the law to handle the matter, they may listen to you. Jungle justice cannot bear good fruits."

"Chief, the rebels were merciless towards us, why should we show them mercy? Mammy Nana queried. "No animal turns on its kind with such purposeless cruelty" I retorted.

The chief clears his throat. "I want all of you to listen carefully. Close to half-a-million people have been affected by this war either through death of their loved ones, displacement, maiming or mutilation, or loss of property. If all these close-to-half-a-million people chose to mete out jungle justice on their suspected or proven offenders, what do you think will happen? Total chaos: no more, no less."

"So, are you saying they should go free?" I retorted.
He offers no reply.

"At the moment you have over forty thousand offenders being clothed, fed and sheltered under the umbrella of the Disarmament, Demobilization and Reintegration Programme. Why? Why are the victims left to look after themselves? It's not fair!" Mammy Nana screamed out in frustration and anger.

"It will be madness to send all those people to jail," the chief replies calmly. "Besides those still in the bush will just continue to fight. Don't you want the war to end?"

"It will end after my revenge!"

"Do you mean that after about half a million people would have had their revenge? You may not like to hear this, but most of these fighters are victims of circumstances, of a rotten system. Most of them just got caught up in this horrible mess. We must give them another chance to a normal life."

Scarcely had he finished making this last statement than the townspeople returned with the rebels. But I notice that the town's people are subdued. Soon I learn why. The leader of the gang, the man I have been praying to God to hand over to me for nine good months, is pushed forward so that I can do whatever I wish with him. To my dismay, I find out that the leader of the gang facing me is Braima, my own son. He had always been wayward, never loved school, and loved money to a fault, but I have always believed he had a warm and generous heart. We were all fond of him despite his faults. Jebbeh was terribly upset when we learned that he had been captured and was devastated when we heard rumours that he had been killed. For all his faults, never in my wildest imagination had I thought he would have the heart to lead a troop to attack his own town, ending up

55

spilling his own blood. What I am experiencing at this moment is a terrible feeling beyond imagination.

The huge young man roars, "Mammy Nana, we are waiting for your orders; your wish will be our command".

I look at my son, I look in his eyes. I have never seen so much misery and remorse written on anyone's face as it was on my son's, but his crime was unforgivable.

"Mama," Braima pleads desperately in a hoarse voice. "I had no choice. I would have been killed and still the attack would have gone ahead as planned. I was hoping that the news of the impending attack would reach you before we got here. I did try to warn you by firing a few shots in the air before we got here. I almost got killed for that. Mama, Jebbeh, Papa, I'm sorry. Please forgive me. I'm ready to take any punishment as long as you forgive me."

I turn my back on my only son, "Take him away from here, and do whatever you wish to do with him, but please take him away! I don't want to see his face ever again."

"Mama!" my son groans. The sound is like a sharp knife stuck to my heart. It is Jebbeh, whose only daughter was killed, with perhaps little chance of giving birth to another, who runs to his brother and embraces him and kisses him, all over his dirty tear-stained emaciated face. They hold each other and weep: my daughter and my son, one forgiving, the other repentant; one merciful, the other remorseful. It is a sight moving enough to stir a mountain.

Indeed, it stirred more than a mountain because my husband, paralyzed for nine months, miraculously got to his feet! To our amazement, my husband took a few faltering steps forward and then got down the two short steps of our veranda and walked unsteadily to where his daughter and his wayward son were weeping in each other's arms and embraced them. I wept and so did my husband. The chief took out a handkerchief ostensibly to wipe his sweating brow, but actually wiped tears from his eyes. The huge town man's eyes misted, and he walked away embarrassed to have displayed such feminine emotion publicly. Two tough-looking rebels broke down and wept uncontrollably.

Then, slowly and quietly, the crowd dispersed, leaving us with our wayward son to recover from this unforgettable encounter.

Gbanabom Hallowell

TOO LOUD FOR A SOCCER MATCH

I had two concerns as I stepped out my door at 8:30 that morning to visit her at her home. I wondered if she would ask me just to lie face up in the bed, while she elicited pleasure from my body as she always insisted, and whether she would also demand that I stay with her all day in the green lagoon of her lust, while her husband was busy establishing himself in the new Republic of Chaos? Both prospects discomforted me. For one thing, whenever Mrs. Gimi More entangled me in her being, she pulled, twisted and tore all over me with such violence that I ended up a victim of her desire. In those moments, she was a woman ridding herself of a pain put in her body long ago by someone who was supposed to be her *real* man.

Mrs. Gimi More provided me with no food all day. She used the flimsy excuse that going in and out of the room would alert her neighbours, who often came to her doorstep asking for a mortar and a pestle to pound their yams, or for leaves and salt for their broths, as if she was the epitome of domesticity. Besides, she would say, what about the prospect of someone discovering me in her bedroom?

In my unpredictable anger, I had tried to warn her that by not providing me food to eat in the interim of lovemaking, my guts would be in such pain that I would be unable to continue making love to her. Since she had never paid any attention to my complaints, I had learned to get my fill to

58

the brim with the cheap food sold at a local slum cookery stall with the allowances she gave me before I honoured her nagging invitations. If the truth was to be known, I also visited the stall because it was a centre for people's gossip – a local information centre.

The Mammy Felleh Cookery Shop leaned considerably to one side with age and neglect until all the zinc ripped into shreds across it like lightning in the sky. The Harmattan wind beat a perpetual noise out of the structure, causing customers to shout their orders, so they could be heard.

"Do, mɛk a gɛt rɛs ɛn kasada lif!" was regularly re-echoed by three or four customers before the large Mammy Felleh or one of her two aides responded. Conversations of many kinds popped up along the counter from the people waiting to have their orders filled. There was talk of credits and debits, of household disputes, of lovers, friends and foes of sports and athletics. There were stories about the good old days and hard times. Eventually, all the talk drifted to a common topic: the sorrow and suffering brought about by the war.

Ours were the longest lunch breaks I had ever had. We were the unemployed and ne'er-do-wells. Our judicial structure had a loaded agenda of state matters. Most pervasive was the corruption of elected officials and other public hangers-on, not fit, according to collective opinion, to run the country. However, this was gossip that I did not like to be a party to. Someone would eventually pick a topic that was directly related to me while I sat there, unable to say a thing in response.

Just as I had feared, someone had always mentioned Gig. I did not like to talk about Gig and the vigilante group in public. I was a part of this vigilante that Gig headed, the only militia that the government and the police recognised as having a legitimate right to patrol greater Freetown in the townships of Waterloo, Tombo, Hastings, Funkia and Adonkia in this time of war. This assignment was created after the guerilla rebels fighting the government for the past four years in the hinterlands had sent a letter to the government saying that they were ready to attack Freetown; the government needed a militia group to help the military in guarding the city.

It took thirty minutes to get the 'rice and cassava leaves' that I had ordered. I always requested a large brass spoon that allowed me to scoop more than the usual silver spoon did. I believe I was the only university graduate with first-class honours degree visiting that place. Had I succeeded in my last interview which I had attended, dressed with a tie and a waistcoat, I could have bid farewell to Mammy Felleh's cheap BLD: Breakfast, Lunch, and Dinner. Again, like my previous interviews, Mrs. Gimi More had put in a word at the wrong time and to the wrong person. A former college mate of mine, who happened to have been a relative of Mrs. Gimi More's contact person, won the job, regardless of his third-class degree and lack of experience. How did I come to know that? I ran into him one lunch hour. He was dressed in a necktie and waistcoat and he was headed for GEM, an expensive Lebanese-owned tourist restaurant for lunch. After a few courtesies in which he had cleverly included his impressive new job description, which, by the way, he knew I myself had applied for, he entered into its air-conditioned interior. I was left standing in front of the restaurant's tinted glass door. It was the nearest I had been to GEM. As I stood outside looking in, the tinted windows reflected my disheveled sweat-soaked image. When I saw myself, I quickly tucked my shirt into my trousers and put myself together in a manner befitting a university product who, even in the time of my economic adversity, should not forget that I was a vanguard of every positive allusion. Without regard to my presence, the glass door rudely flew open, flinging my image aside, as though some secret arbiter of social standards had pulled it away from the restaurant. From the open door, there issued a small knot of wild, attractive young girls, the sort that I had always dreamed of having in bed instead of Mrs. Gimi More.

The Mammy Felleh Cookery Shop suddenly became very crowded. People kept streaming in by the front and side doors. Some of us who had finished our meals delayed our exit from the facility for the obvious reason of being idle. Others ordered more food. A stench hung in the air. The zinc structure like the people it housed was wet, and so was the floor. Once again, the crowd cried out, *"kasada lif!"* followed by the loud clanking of plates and spoons and the scorching call for *"wata!"* to drink. Responding to the cries, a child sauntered through the crowd with a container, and announced the cost per polythene.

In addition, two other children added to the refrain, *"Cold Ice!"* The redundant phrase informed buyers that it was not just cold water they had: they were selling unthawed ice; therefore, it came with a higher price. Opposite where I sat were two big fellows, who were known for calling out for service every other hour. Currently, they sat over their empty plates talking loudly to each other. The crowd thought their conversation was interesting and so a large number were drawn into listening or contributing to it. I was one of those.

Each time Mrs. Gimi More crossed my mind with her passion for wild sex, my desire for reordering lunch grew. Food soon became a weapon to subdue eroticism.

"Did you guys hear that Gig has ordered the stadium officials to cancel all soccer matches?" one of the big fellows asked. He was known as Extro, short for extrovert. His partner was Intro, short for introvert. Those who knew them well did not need to be reminded that the pair hated those names like hell. One felt tarnished by the sobriquet; the other felt affronted.

"And who is this Gig to cancel a soccer match just like that? Has he got anything against the sport?" said a frail man, licking his spoon like a starving dog, and straining his neck to closely observe Extro and Intro.

Extro turned to look in his direction. He might have slapped the frail man if he had been closer.

"What are you talking about? Do you know who Gig is?" Extro grunted.

"I know he is not a sports official, to say the least," the frail man replied. "Otherwise…"

"Otherwise? Otherwise what?" Extro growled.

The frail man did not like Extro's demented look. He shifted his empty plate before him and belched so hard that the crowd burst out into laughter. Extro felt better.

"The Eagles soccer team cannot come for the match because the rebels have blocked the Freetown-Kono highway," Extro continued from where the frail man had interrupted him, looking around to make sure we all made sense of what he was saying.

"So, you are saying Gig warned match officials that the Kono team wouldn't come to Freetown because of the rebel roadblock?" said the frail man, undaunted.

Intro, who had not said anything until then, shouted him down.

But the frail man persisted. "It couldn't have been Gig who cancelled the soccer match," he said.

"Then, who did?" asked Intro.

"Only the government has such power," said the frail man.

Two or three other people who had merely been listening to the exchange now chimed in to tell the frail man he was being a nuisance. Intro then went on to tell him who Gig was, just in case the frail man had suddenly materialised from God-knows-where. He told the man that a vigilante commander like Gig sat in every security and social committee, sometimes even as chairman or secretary. We began to wonder what this frail man was really interested in anyway.

Was it the cancelled soccer match or Gig?

Who was he by the way?

Was he a rebel spy among us?

Everyone wanted to know.

During the war, to be branded a rebel in the city of Freetown was to be made a prey to mob justice. There was the story of a boy who snatched a purse from a helpless woman in a crowded marketplace. The chase took the two of them into meandering streets, but only the woman worked up a sweat. She began losing her attacker until she had the sense to shout, "Rebel! Rebel!" Almost automatically, the entire street took chase. The boy, aware of the stake and the furnace awaiting his apprehension,

protested. "I'm a thief, not a rebel!" he cried. "I am a thief, not a rebel! I stole her purse. Here it is!"
"If you don't know, Gig has his eyes everywhere," said Intro, who still had the floor. "Just turn your oversized head and see who is watching over your thick skull." Intro spoke not to threaten, but to caution.

I was not surprised. Anyone could identify me. Every vigilante member was nearly as well-known as Gig himself. I was embarrassed that with all my education I should be associated with the abstract nature of violence, so that the frail man had to be on his guard at all times, fearful of speaking his mind. The consensus was that I could either physically humble him or pass a command to achieve the same.

The poor man turned and grinned into my face. I quickly turned away.
"You want to be a big mouth? Badamaci will teach you a lesson," Extro growled.
"All right, all right," the frail man said.
It was my turn to inquire who these big bullies were that knew my name. Why hadn't I left after I'd had lunch? Everyone's concentration shifted from the frail man to me. Had I quickly responded to Mrs. Gimi More's invitation after eating, I would have been saved from the embarrassment of this moment. I was always proud to be identified as one of Gig's henchmen. I felt elated to be considered in the company of his closest boys: Kabila, Shaka Zulu, and Fidel Castro, boys who had almost lost their real names in the inferno of the war. They were so popular by their adopted names that I thought of getting one myself, like Winston Churchill. I would then keep

Badamaci for use in purely academic circles and yes, for the comfort of Mrs. Gimi Moore, who thought my name meant a Bad Man with No Mercy.

However, she only told me so whenever I turned down her invitation for sex. But when she was feeling horny, she would say, "Do you know what your name stands for? Do you?" She would breathe hard into her telephone and almost grunting, she would answer her own question. "Your name stands for Bad Man—Have Mercy—on a starving woman who cannot run around like your little girls. That's it. That's what your name stands for, loving darling. Are you going to come?"

"I'll only stop by...I'm not myself today," I usually replied.

"You're going to be just fine, just fine. You just stop by for a while."

"Bro," someone in the crowd addressed Extro with ghetto respect. "Is the match really cancelled? I cannot wait to see the Eagles' defense in the field of play. To get past that defense with a ball is like breaking through a wall. The boys have the wall. You can't just shoot past them all; no matter how hard you dribble the ball."

"You must be talking history," Extro began. "That was before, when the Eagles had a player like Koboko as their main back. Ever since he got scrapped in their last match with the Lions, their defense tumbled down like the great Berlin wall. However, making for that loss is the strength of their center forward. Ooh! They have the best center forward I know. No need for their defense to sweat."

"Super, for the best center forward, you are surely looking in the wrong direction." Intro, who supported another team, begged to differ with his partner.

"Let's hear what you have on your list," Extro taunted as if whispering to someone, but he spoke loud enough to be heard on the town square. He said, "Now let's hear what Fisheries can do. I know that's your team."

"You want to know the truth?" asked Intro.

"Well, let's hear the truth according to the Fisheries team supporter," Extro responded.

"The truth is that every good spectator knows that Fisheries has the best center forward set-up today, and not just because I'm a fan," Intro countered. He obviously had considerable support from the audience.

The football subject brought a friendly disposition to the crowd, eliminating every tension and fear. Players individually came under scrutiny with solid analyses of their performances as well as goal they have scored and number of appearances. There was talk of the international trading of players. A disagreement about who was the most expensive Sierra Leonean soccer player divided the crowd. Even though Extro insisted on a particular player, his choice did not make the first five in the arguable best. For one thing, there were no reliable statistics to support anyone's claim. Someone cautioned that no one should trust the figures appearing in the local dailies: how could reporters, who had never obtained visas to a European country, know about the contractual fees of oversea players? Add this to the fact that the players themselves do not usually want their earnings disclosed to the general public, and then you get a better understanding of the farce about journalism in this country today.

Another voice dismissed all the comments as rubbish. "What with the explosion of the Internet," he said, "the local teams that originally owned the traded players always know about such contracts, and they feel proud about publishing the financial worth of their players to attract new talents to their clubs."

"You gƐt IntanƐt? You know IntanƐt?" a rather mucky voice asked from the back, but it could not be put with a face.

"This stupid war raging over our heads is depriving us of good football," said the frail man, again bursting with anxiety. "How is this country supposed to discover new talents? This useless war has not allowed us to see a professional football match in a long time. Now look at the stadium lying dormant. Morale is down, and every good player is going abroad. Today, there are more Sierra Leonean players in one foreign team than in any one team in the country."

The frail man earned himself some respect again with his outburst, which received a standing ovation. He continued to talk about the state of world football, to other sports, like basketball and how the latter is thriving well in the United States.

From deep within the crowd the mucky voice came up again. *"You dↄn go de? You know America?"*

This question provoked a brief laughter before the silence returned. Resuming, the frail man said that because the United States did not show much interest in what he called "international soccer" and was not financing it, the football World Council, FIFA, was finding it difficult to promote the sport the way it should be.

Another man in the crowd took the reference to the United States as an opportunity to veer off on a tangent. "The United States never honours its debt owed to the UN because it wants the UN destroyed," the man said.

A towering figure nearby jumped in. "You think that America cannot pay its debts. America is the richest and most powerful country in the world," he literally shouted out.

Another voice cried, "Why won't America pay its debts then, if it is so powerful?"

The crowd disagreed for a while about America being a shallow bigmouth and a country trying to boss the rest of the world around.

"It is not called America; it is called the United States of America," the mucky voice shouted again.

Another feat of laughter followed.

"What's the difference?" the previous speaker questioned.

Looking around, Extro came down heavily on the man's leg like a dictator, reminding the others they were not there to discuss America or the United States of America, or whatever it was called, just football. He urged the frail man to continue his explanation.

As if to prevent further trouble, the frail man shifted his focus to Brazil. He spoke for five minutes about Pele, whom he called by his little known original name, Edson Arantes do Nascimento, and particularly about his recent role as a politician in the sports affairs of his country. He then turned to Europe where, he said, "Football rests its head on fine pillows."

He spoke about why hooliganism in football matches was as European as a cup of tea. Regarding the many African football stars going off to play for European teams, he said it was an African reversal of power base. In other words, it was African colonialism of the west. He then went on to establish an unclear theory of why black people were excelling in sports more than any other race. Then he rested his case.

He had successfully stolen the show from the big fellows, who had little to say about international football.

Everyone agreed the war had destroyed most of Sierra Leone's institutions.

The war had been raging for four years now. People seemed to be slithering like a snake on a smooth surface, with a conspicuous inability to forge ahead. When the war first broke out, people were still attending football matches, but with guns all over the place, players and spectators were shot, football officials lost their money, and the whole institution was stuck rotating only on an undecided trust.

It occurred to me that the football and war situations were similar to the one between Mrs. Gimi More and I. There had never been a relationship per se, at least as far as I knew it. I enjoyed the union, but it was she who did all the groaning. There were times I looked in the mirror and said to myself, "Badamaci, sex is a gainless labour." Then for a while, I resisted every temptation that came my way. However, after a few days of celibacy, I missed her and began to smolder with a fresh fire. I was like a starved spectator, wishing for a good match.

For me, sex had become not just an appetite that lingered on among young men of my generation, but a survival skill. During the war, brothels were converted into royal houses with young peasants like me, rising to kiss the lips of princesses. In war, as in football, people talk about attack, defense, retreat, and advance. No matter how you looked at it, sex was a type of war, and all I came away from the university with was the instinct to survive on it. With an old hand like Mrs. Gimi More, I was caught up in a primordial web, like a graduate of books.

69

In our war, an unmarried woman became Miss-Hard-to-Get, or was it Miss-Hard-to-Meet? These young spinsters were mostly in the hands of men in authority, who had grown tired of their own wives. The starving lots were married women. At night they littered the streets in the nude, under the pretext of saving their children from running off to become guerilla combatants, but they ended in the embrace of men, the age of their children. Mrs. Gimi More often told me I made her remember the lost youth in her husband without dreaming of growing gray. When I listened to her groaning on top of me, she told me how her husband was busy creating a place for himself in the larger republic, I could not help thinking how our war of polychromatic anger was all about failed relationships.

It wasn't Gig who had brought me into the vigilante movement. I had been dribbled as a ball into it by the wind of unemployment. Originally I had opted for the military, but it was stretched. Resources were low. The government needed more enlisted men than it needed officers. In addition, the reality was that the government was at ease recruiting children whom they paid nothing. As one government official told me, adding that it was for my ears only, "We are sending the equals of our enemy's child soldiers to war. On the other side, they have children who march into war with no reservations. Our adult soldiers have their wives to think about. Many of them have perished at the hands of children. The children we send to war are our only saviours." In my case, the official advised me to linger in the government approved vigilante group to wait for the end of what he called, "this recklessness." A note to Gig made it possible. Gig had taken a liking to me at once. He always took me around with him, making me

70

draft reports and write correspondences for him to sign. Some weekends he invited me to drink beer at his place. A vigilante may be a volunteer, but I was never a soldier in reserve. I did not have to be on the front-line of the war front, although I carried a licensed weapon along the streets in my neighborhood by day and by night.

We ignited bonfires in the compound of those we protected, sang songs of bravery, activities that were enhanced by guns, alcohol, and marijuana. One day, an angry old woman said to me, "You boys are doing well by protecting us, but to sing into our ears in the dead of night is to have us carry the war into our meagre sleep. God save us!" Immediately, I thought she was being ungrateful. I looked into her eyes with the anger of a completely dry spirit and spelled for her W-A-R backwards. I told her that was what we were. Moreover, I added, "God save the Queen and her husband. God save the monarchy. God save colonialism, post-colonialism, and anti-colonialism. God save the military and God save the military's alter-ego, the vigilantes. God save the perpetrator. God save the victim. God save other gods." I meant to make her look irrelevant. She looked into my face with the bitter aspect of elderly conceit and said she wished she could trade places with the dead. When I offered to help her achieve her wish, she cried like a baby.

The community complained about me to Gig. Gig visited our camp, and with one long look at me, he decided I had what it took to lead a unit. He told me that he wanted to put some sense into my head for that new role. I told him I already had enough of it with honors I had received from the university. He tapped me on my back and said it was a shame that my country could not find a dignified place for me, with all my learning.

"It's all right," I told him. "All of us are displaced anyway."

Gig was a man with a soaring ambition. Once he told me his dreams were complex even for his own comprehension. He liked to talk late into the night. He never drank alcohol, but he was addicted to coffee. Gig did not believe himself to be a soldier. The weight of an AK 47 on his back made him stoop. He shook like a reed when a cold wind blew. He was always scared to death when, for instance, a tyre burst into flames. Moreover, the thought of war unnerved him. In fear, the first thought that came to him was of his family: his wife first and then his only child, whom he had managed to send to live with his sister in England. Whenever he was leaving a place, he always remembered to pick up his mug but forgot his gun, even if it was lying right in front of him. A few weeks later, he paid the ultimate price for that habit. Gig was a diamond in the rough. He thought himself a diamond because as a young man, he was aware of his potential. He had always wanted the best for a country that had gained independence at the same time as he had. His father had told him on his twentieth birthday that he was a grown man, and therefore was free to go out into the heart of the country by himself, "Now that the British have given us a breathing space to properly own our country," his father had said. Heeding his father's advice, Gig had gone and kept going into the heart of the country. He told me that maybe, at mid-life; he had gone too deep or too blindly to be of any more use to himself.

"I'm always troubled by my fratricidal countrymen whom we have made into leaders," he said. "When our freedom-founding fathers wanted the British to go, they complained a lot about the injustices of colonialism and the enslavement of the black mind. No sooner were they in control than they began nurturing violence toward each other."

He paused and sipped heavily from his coffee. "Every young man then needed a role model," he said. "We looked up to those of our elders who, during the white man's rule, had gone abroad and educated themselves. But when they had returned, they fell below our expectations and allowed their differences to manipulate them. When I look back, I pity their blindness to the historical significance of their era. In their foolishness, they had inflicted wounds in our hearts." He buried his head for a while and when he raised it; his eyes were as red as the setting sun. "I have a duty to turn this system around for young minds like yours."

The war had taken considerable energy from Gig. He depended on his stoicism, along with what little substance was left in him, to run the affairs of the vigilantes. That night was the closest I ever came to him. Although he threw his power all over the place, it was his stoic ghost that did all the talking. Thereafter, it was not unusual for the two of us to sit down away from the bonfire with the night-spell off our brows and talk about the ways of the world. A tyre exploding in the furnace made him jump, splattering coffee all over himself. He whispered his wife's name and that of his child. He drank heavily from his mug with a nervous hand.

"I came into this to save my country, but already my own life is pushing too hard on me," Gig said, almost in solitary conversation with his mug. "I know the rebels will attempt to come to Freetown. I must warn you, Badamaci." He turned to me and said, "Watch yourself, and watch your neighbour. In times like these, a man reaps what he sows.

73

The government does not trust the national army any longer. There have been too many renegade soldiers, more than enough to start a platoon. Watch yourself, if you want to grow old. I am doing this for my family. I love my wife a great deal, but I notice the war has taken a lot of her from me."

He turned towards me again, and after a moment I realised that he was staring intently, eyeing me longer than he ever did, almost as though he wanted to stab my eyes. I remained silent. "After all this madness," he continued, "I will go into the forests, mountains, and rivers to rescue her." He paused and took a heavy sip of his coffee. I could hear his throat gulping. "Badamaci, do you make love to a woman with a complete forgetfulness of any state of affair?"

The question did not sink in properly, but I grunted. He took that as an answer, but I did not know whether he had taken it as a "yes" or a "no." I waited until he removed his flask from his knapsack, refilled his mug, took a sip, and threw his gaze, perhaps his very mind, into the fire.

"Did you just ask whether I make love with . . .?"

"Never mind," he waved a hand. "If you had made love during your university days and still came out with first-class honors while your colleagues sweated their asses over their books for nothing, what other state of affairs, especially one during a war time like this, could matter to you? Maybe one theory you might like to expand on in your future learning is that the best time to make love to a woman is during moments of tension, when every pain has been achieved. You exploit her feminine vulnerability.

"Think of all the wars you have read about," he said. The world wars, *Napoleonic wars, Hitler's war,* the *Burma war* in which Sierra Leoneans fought. The other day I was talking with old Corporal Kargbo, who himself fought in the *Burma war*. I wanted him to help us manage the vigilantes, but all that is in his head is the memory of the young Asian girls he fucked by the dozens. Do you know that pain prolongs a man's pleasure?

"Every brutal act, whether by soldiers or rebels, has been interspersed with romance, and the reverse is not always the case. In civilian terms, the fighter's romance is only known as rape. I have heard of rebels raping corpses. There was a rebel who was so touched by the beauty of a corpse he chanced upon in the nude; he carried her on his shoulder fifteen miles and hid her in a derelict house. It is alleged that he made love to her every other hour. After a while, he declared to his colleagues that he had discovered the African Nomoli, whose beauty outclassed the Italian Madonna. Well, of course he didn't mention the Italian Madonna by name, but when he said, 'more beautiful than all of God's creation' he meant the Italian Madonna, Beersheba, every Egyptian queen, Nefertiti, Marilyn Monroe, and Romeo's Juliet. He told his squad mates that she was a fresh corpse with the silence of one who will be resurrected after every painful fandango. One day after the sun had fallen behind the huge black hills, he shut her up in the house, protecting the only door and window with stones and trees. He urged his colleagues to do the right thing. He was going on the road. He would be the urgent revolutionary, and in so doing, would save the only known Nomoli. She was destined to be resurrected at the end of the war to produce new virgins and romantic saints, who would in turn make the world a better place. Marching like a Neanderthal, the rebel went into the hottest part of the battle and was never heard from again."

I hiccupped when I did not hear him talk again. The bonfire was dimming a few meters away. In the darkness, he sipped heavily at his coffee. I wanted to ask him many questions, but I could not break his silence. I wanted to know what happened to the African Nomoli. What kind of spirit took possession of the young man? Why would he mess with a dead woman? It was as though Gig read my thoughts.

He said, "The woman was not dead, she was only a corpse." He sounded heavier in this single utterance than he had in his entire disturbing story. I wanted to tell him how much he was torturing my mind, but when I looked away from the fire, he had gone into the night. I shamefully acknowledged that Gig had put a lot of sense into my university head.

The next day I entered the Mammy Felleh Cookery Shop only to find it cold and silent. Only three people were sitting there. Two were at one end, and a lonely man sat near the door. Nobody was eating, although it was way into lunchtime. One thing I knew, because I ate there every day, was that something was not right for the Mammy Felleh Cookery Shop to be so cold and silent at a time like that. I began to wonder whether the proprietress had fallen ill. But I would have heard about her from the people I met.

My mind went back to the last accusation she suffered in the local dailies. It was alleged she ground dried goat shit on the hard skin of a seashell and washed it with the ink of koranic surahs written on a tablet, in her pots of broth to attract customers. The report had threatened her business, but after she tactfully began advertising on television, the crowd had gradually returned and eventually grown to such overwhelming proportions as she had never seen before.

It was that prodigal crowd of customers that had brought along the two big fellows and the frail man. Nobody knew where they had come from, and everyone knew they were not from our community. However, they had soon become known and respected in their different ways. None of them was a member of the vigilante movement, and it surprised me that men as robust as the two big fellows did not become a part of our group. Although the two big fellows were known to be boisterous, all they argued about was football. Extro had fought on two occasions with people who had dared to openly disagree with him. The good beatings he had given them had sent ripples into the spine of everyone. The frail man became known as Socrates, because he always had something strange to say about faraway places.

I saw Mammy Felleh coming out of her kitchen.
"What's the matter? Mammy Felleh, have you ran out of food?" I asked.
"No," she answered, "I have run out of customers. What is it about football that is making you men crazy?" she asked, examining her lunch bowls.
"My answer, Mammy Felleh, is I want to eat very good food before any football player comes here."
We both laughed.
"Well, it seems they are really going to play football here today and if they are so worked out, my food will sell well."
"How is that? How come?
" I asked.
"You have not heard? You are the only one I know who doesn't have the fever."
"Why? I heard that lunch is ready, and I'm starving with the flu."

"If you haven't heard, the Eagles are going to turn the city upside down today. You'd better braced yourself for the match."

"The Eagles are coming down to Freetown! I can't believe this."

"You better do; I understand that Gig gave the okay last night to the sports officials, and come to think about it, you should know about that. It has been arranged that the Kono team will come to Freetown today. You can see this place is empty because everyone is on the highway to welcome the team."

Just then the distant shout of exuberance drifted in with the wind, reverberating like the passion of the ocean tide crashing on concave banks.

"That," Mammy Felleh said, hesitating, *"is too loud for a soccer match."*

"Only, if we don't win. I hope the scores are good for us," I said as I moved off.

When I stepped outside of the Mammy Felleh Cookery Shop, a jubilant scene greeted me. Taxi drivers had little flags on the sides of their bonnets bearing the colours and logos of the teams they supported. They blasted their car horns. The radio station was running a pre-analysis of the match. The streets were rife with arguments.

"Let the match begin!"

"I am thirsty for professional football. Let it play!"

"Bet my watch in favour of the Eagles!" one bystander offered to another, unstrapping his gold watch.

"I bet my best watch for Lions!" another unstrapped his silver coloured watch.

"First goal by the Eagles, I bet my gold chain!"

"First goal by Lions, I bet chain for chain!"
Gig, approved the match! How was he able to get the Eagles to hit the road, a road we knew the president had commanded barricaded to frustrate a rebel attack into Freetown? I turned the question over repeatedly in my mind.

When I walked up to the highway, I saw that it was lined with expectant people for a mile. The sun had gone down for a drink, where the Rokel stitched with the Atlantic Ocean. Nobody expected it would suddenly come back up in the sky. Quenched, it would just go to bed. The police had tried to disperse the crowd, but they had failed. They now busied themselves with diverting traffic. When I saw many familiar faces red with expectation and with no need for *kasada lif*, I pitied Mammy Felleh's great loss. Street bars blasted heavy music, while men and women sat in them and gulped beers. Children grouped in teams and played backyard football with larger than life names coming to their lips.

"Pass it to me, Pele!"
"Ball here, Maradona!"
"Kick it to me, Roger Miller."

I dismissed them after I realised they were grouping into backyard teams a whole history of world football, of stars born in different countries and in different generations. Dogs, the mangy and the rabid, barked at passers-by in a torment, known only to them. I raised my eyes to the outskirts of the city and saw the hills crouched in dark muteness. Perhaps, only the dogs knew at that moment that the land was still at war.

I saw the two big fellows leading a mammoth crowd of celebrants on Kissy Road. They arrived at the Upgun

Junction where many years ago, the British had mounted their cannons to repel a possible French invasion from neighboring Guinea into colonial Freetown. The crowd was divided into two factions that fell into a long line on either side of the road. Choruses rang out long and loud. The waiting had been long, but the crowd's expectation hadn't been daunted. Before it sank into the ocean, the last ray of the sun had blazed as though lulled by the choruses. A little later, the black dust of night hung in the insalubrious air. The peeping eyes of hurricane lamps were awakened on the edges of street stalls. Occasionally, bright beams of distant headlights glowed before they disappeared off a bend. The crowd continued to endure. Beleaguered hopes could be faintly heard in the dark.

"They will come," said one man in the crowd. "They are on their way. They don't have to play until tomorrow evening, so they have all the time they need to arrive tonight. They will surely arrive in Freetown tonight."

"My Eagles will come with claws ready for the grasp!" another said.

"Come on, Eagles, the Lions will show you what they are made of!"

"Fly, fly, and fly, Eagles of the sky, the people hunger for a game!"

"Roar, roar, and roar, Lions of the jungle, and wake up the gods from their lazy beds!"

Suddenly, a blast cut across the impenetrable darkness, whistling with ineluctable power. An abrupt silence followed. Stillness seized every breath. A second blast spat, like breaking china, shattered the air behind the hills. In the eerie silence an eternal voice screamed,

"Dɛm dɔ n kam!"

"'Dɛ m dɔ n kam!"

The crowd merged into one being, thundering with excitement. It surged to welcome the expected. Blasts ricocheted in the dark with tongues of fire descending on the crowd. Multiple languages cracked from within and the union of one suddenly fragmented. The moments suddenly turned cruel. Yet, the large mass at the rear pressed forward, as a new language of despair emerged from crushed bones ahead. The rebels had entered Freetown!

Flashes continued to cut into the darkness, spilling over houses, setting them on fire. The remnants of the crowd gave way, and the rebels merged with them.

Excitement turned into fear. Cheering turned into wailing. Suddenly, death was coiling on everyone's doorsteps. As vigilantes, we were late to respond, but it wasn't hard for us to regroup, since most of us were already together around at the bonfires. Without waiting for a command, we spilled over, poised for action. We didn't have to close in on the rebels; the national army was already on the defensive. The soldiers asked us to comb our neighborhoods for snipers. We felt emasculated by the request until three vigilantes were gunned down from unsuspected windows. Then we became nervous.

A hand pulled me from behind, and I farted in the darkness. I knew I couldn't turn around quickly enough to shoot my attacker, so I sprawled on the ground. The figure slowly came upon me. "Shhhhh," Mrs. Gimi More said.

"Badamaci, I have been searching for you everywhere," she said.

"Don't you see we have been attacked?" The smell of rancid sex came to my nose with hot anger.

81

"I know, I know, but—I have to…it's my husband," she was breathing heavily.

"What about your husband?" I thundered.

"Gig has found out about you and me. And he is mad," she began to cry.

At once I wanted to tell her it was her funeral. But then the thought of Gig's story cut across my mind, and I realised why a female corpse was not necessarily a dead woman. His wife, Mrs. Gimi More, had become a corpse to him. Gig had learned about my affair with his wife before the night he told me the story. *So, the story he had told me was about my undoing; I was the young man who had discovered his wife as the African Nomoli. I was the young man who would be the urgent revolutionary to go to war and never to be heard from again. That's why Gig had said that the war had taken a lot from his wife.*

"What did he say? How did he know about our affair?" I made a show of doubting her statement.

"Oh, Badamaci, Gig knows everything about you and me in the bedroom. Up to and including the number of times we have had sex. He talked with hate about the roughness and stench of the bedcovers," she burst out crying anew.

I could smell the covers too. The sweat running down our joints, the small *Mm* towel we had used to wipe our properties wet with semen. I could hear the noisy fucking on the hard hunch of the bed and feel again our moments of collapse. For the first time I learned why a man would kill for his wife. Mrs. Gimi More cried harder, probably only then, confronting the reality of cheating.

"It will be okay," I told her.

She cried harder. At the same time, the gunfire grew closer. She didn't even seem to be aware of it.

"You have to leave this place now," I said. "It is dangerous for you to be here. You don't want to get shot."

"What about yourself? Let us get away from here."

"I have a task. You have to go at once," I said, merely to get her away from me.

"But I am afraid Gig will hurt me. And I also have something else to tell you."

"And what would that be?"

She hesitated and looked deeply into my eyes. "I want to know whether, you really do love me"

I felt a burning anger at her foolishness. "You know very well that I do," I murmured.

"I don't know that you do, but I'll be satisfied with that."

After a short pause, she took my hand into hers. "Badamaci, can we run away from here?"

"Run away? What do you mean?"

"I have Gig's money with me. I have buried it somewhere. We can go to England or America."

"You have to think about visas," I said muttering the first thing that came to my mind.

"Our money can buy them. With money, you can buy any visa."

"How much money do you think you need?" I tried not to exhibit excitement.

"What can't we have with ten million Leones?"

I tried converting the Leones into dollars, since the Leones had lost considerable value. "Don't tell me that is what you have!"

"That's what Gig handed to me yesterday. I didn't count it, but he told me that's what was in the bag. Wait, he said he had stones in it, but I don't know what they are for."

"Where is the bag?"

"I have buried it somewhere."

83

"You know—please, first let us save your life. We shall talk when this battle is contained."

After a while I was able to convince her to seek refuge at the Mammy Felleh Cookery Shop, where I promised to meet her later. I knew I was supposed to be a combatant in this battle, but later in the dark, I stole away from the action. The night pumped hot air into me. I hesitated for a moment, surveying the chaos around me. Mrs. Gimi More ran on ahead. In fear that she might get too far ahead of me, I began to move toward the Mammy Felleh Cookery Shop again. Then, suddenly, the world (or my world) stood still. I heard Gig calling me from behind. I couldn't make him out in the dark, for he held a brilliant torch toward me. It took a while for me to realise that when he called out, *"friidg,"* he meant that I should stay still (or freeze!) He began to move towards me.

"You could get killed for being careless," he said.

There was calmness in his voice, but it was pregnant with rage.

"Why are you stealing away from action? You wanted to be an officer in the army, and I trusted you. Do you enjoy being a thief? Running away from action is molestation to the quick and the dead. Didn't you learn that in the university? If you were a child of God, you would know why Christ took those nails. However, you are too sectarian to be able to understand why a man doesn't fornicate with war. You are a disgrace to your country. How many times have I asked you to provide leadership? Of course, without morals there can be no leadership."

I boiled within.

"Gig is mad," I recalled Mrs. Gimi More saying to me. I began to defend myself. "I didn't do…"

"I have not asked you!" he shouted. "Sheeet!" I heard the long drag of his American slang. The dim figure behind the bright hot torch seemed to be searching for something on his body. "Where did I put it?"

I knew at once that he had left his gun somewhere, and that he confronted me with only his mug, filled with black coffee. I also knew that he intended to shoot me in cold blood. I suddenly remembered every act of brutality taught to me at the university: Hitler gassing the Jews in Germany, the creative genocide meted out to Fyodor Dostoevsky's peasants in Russia, the slaughterhouse of Idi Amin in Uganda, America condemning its black souls to lynching, the British efforts at wiping the Aborigines from the face of the earth in Australia. It dawned on me that killing others is not so much about hating them as it is about self-preservation. You could even say, "May your soul rest in perfect peace," before disfiguring someone. I cocked my gun, shut my eyes, and squeezed the trigger. When I opened my eyes, I saw his torch on the ground. I took it and turned its dancing light onto a motionless Gig.

Yellow flames loomed from housetops, licking with the thirst of the dry throats of the beasts of hell. I, once again, made my way toward the Mammy Felleh Cookery Shop. Nothing prepared me for the destruction there. Bundles of zinc were melted to the ground as dying flints sprang wildly about. I pointed the torch over the bodies sprawling around. Among them I found Mammy Felleh, the two big fellows, and my university colleague, who ate his lunch at the expensive Gem restaurant. My university colleague died wearing his waistcoat, with his necktie twisted behind his back. What was he doing at Mammy Felleh's? Someone was limping ahead. I flashed the light in that direction, but was unable to see who it was. Just then, the figure stopped.

"Shoot me, Gig! Kill me! I am the only one standing alive that knows you are a rebel spy. You will perish in hell for the people killed because of your football-scam-trap. You will roast in hell, rebel!"

The laconic voice went silent for a while as its owner continued limping away. The dim figure looked back over its shoulder again. The voice came very much like an echo this time.

"And you know what will happen? Badamaci will fuck your woman in the mouth on top of your grave!"

I thrust Gig's torch forward and saw the frail man moving away down the road.

I followed him. Occasionally he disappeared around a bend in the road. However, because he limped I was soon able to close the gap between us. He did not look back again, even though the firing continued behind us both. Though I was still baffled about the connection between Gig and the frail man, I recalled all that had happened in the day. Innocent and useful lives like that of Mammy Felleh that had been lost. I also wondered what could have happened to the football team from Kono. Then, I recalled the argument at the cookery shop. I remembered the two big fellows had agreed that the Eagles team was indeed a good team. No wonder tickets were sold out before noon. And now, here was the frail man talking about my relationship with Gig's wife. I still couldn't connect it all.

The frail man collapsed in the dark but quickly picked himself up again. I noticed he was dragging his left leg, and struggled to pull it along with his left hand. When I saw his condition, I hurried to close the remaining distance between us. Soon, I nearly ran into him. I was close enough to touch him before I realised that he had stopped walking. He turned around to look at me. I flashed the torch on his face.

"No, no, Gig, you are not going to kill me because you need the stones. You can't have them from a dead man," he collapsed on the road again.

"What are you talking about, Socrates?" I shouted.

"Who is this?" he sat up.

"My name is Badamaci."

He touched my hand and said, "I know you. His torch, Gig's torch, how did you get it?"

I did not answer. I led him to the side of the road and helped him sit on a rock. He breathed heavily, but his strength seemed to be returning to him. He winced when he tried to move his left leg. He groaned and cussed. He asked me to hold the torch near his wound. A bullet had ripped his flesh, leaving a jagged tear. His blood ran all the way to his toes.

"Gig is trying to kill me," he said.

He told me that he and Gig had grown up together in the same house, which the frail man called a family house. Socrates may not have been a successful carpenter by urban standards, but he and his family were able to live hand-to-mouth in their small village. A year ago, Gig began to send urgent messages for him to visit him in Freetown.

"The city had frustrated me before, so I had shied away from it," he said.

But Gig had bombarded him with many promises. With the urging of elders in the village, he had left his wife and children behind and had come to visit Gig. Gig was no longer the humble dock worker Socrates had known. He now drove cars with tinted glasses.

"We were all afraid for his lifestyle," Socrates said. "We thought that he was going too deep into corruption, a state of affairs we feared he did not properly understand."

Quiet for a while, Socrates turned to me and said, "Sit down Badamaci, sit down. I have more things to tell you."

I sat on a rock close to him.

Gig had told the frail man he wanted to make him a detective. There were suddenly too many enemies around him. He would be vulnerable to them if he didn't find an extra pair of eyes to watch his back. The frail man was going to be led into a secret only because Gig considered him to be a true brother. Gig had reminded him of the blood bond between them and of the family spirit in both of them. The frail man understood the blood, the spirit, and the ties. He added to them the honour of being asked to benefit from a brother's opportunities.

"Two men are on my trail," Gig had told him.

"Did you say two men are on your trail? What for?" the frail man had asked Gig.

"We are in a war over our heads. You are aware of that, aren't you?"

"But why are two men on *your* trail?" the frail man had pushed. "That's too personal."

"Do you hold your vows of the Poro Society sacred?"

"I hold them sacred, you know that," the frail man had answered, not knowing where the conversation was leading.

"Swear you'll be a man and not a woman in the face of adversity. That you'll die if you reveal."

"Reveal? Reveal what? Where is this going?" Socrates had protested.

"Does a messenger tell a message before or after greeting?"

"It has to be after greeting."

"Well?" Gig asked, having made his point.

The frail man had sworn.

That was why Socrates had been on the trail of the two big fellows. He had secretly followed them wherever they went, listened to what they said, to whom they talked, and, if possible, what they thought. At this point I recalled the argument he'd had with them at Mammy Felleh Cookery Shop. Gig had considered the two big fellows dangerous. He had wanted twenty-four hour surveillance on them. He had provided the frail man with a mobile cell phone that he was to use to call him if anything came up. However, an incident which happened on one particular day made the frail man almost keel over. He had walked into Gig's office and found him and the two big fellows chatting over coffee and beer. When he got over his shock, and after the two big fellows had left, the frail man had told Gig that it was no longer necessary to trail the big fellows.

"Why do you say that? Don't you understand? You have to keep your eyes on them until…"

"Until what… Gig? Are they not supposed to be your friends after the chatting I saw the three of you engaged in?"

"Look here, Socrates. Sit down! I guess I have to make you understand this business better. You see, there is something going on — kind of weird — and you know it is all part of bringing the war to an end. After I became head of the vigilante movement, I received a letter from the rebel leader, Boday Candoh, that he wanted me to broker an agreement between himself and the president, so that they could end the war and form a government of national unity. There is the promise of power and stones: I mean clean diamonds! There is promise of money if I can, you know, help them, I mean the rebels, reach Freetown. And you know what that

89

means for you and the other good people back in the village. The point is that the rebels want to negotiate from a position of strength. They figure if they are in control of half of Freetown, the government will listen to them."

"But, Gig, you know these guys. You know what they are capable of doing."

"Listen, I have been assured that there will be no trouble when they come. Only last week, I advised the president and the Sierra Leone Football Association that the Eagles could be invited for the match that the president had postponed. At the same time, I have assured the rebels that they could surreptitiously come with the team if they promise to open the road on their end a month before the game and not hurt the players and their delegation," he explained.

Back to Extro and Intro, they have been planted on me by the rebels to ensure I was making my promise real."

The frail man suddenly broke off this startling account of the conversation he'd had with Gig. Then I was able to connect the bits to form a whole. I flashed the torch at him. He was pale and weak. He still had his hand on his wound. I offered to carry him on my back, but he declined and said he wanted to talk some more. The guns had almost all gone silent except a few irritating snipers occasionally blasting in the dark. He took my hands into his. I could feel his whole body trembling like that of a very old man. He said he had a confession to make.

"Well, of course I'm not sorry for the first one," he began. "Extro and Intro are dead. They were mutilated by a crowd of civilians. I did what Gig told me to do if they got out of hand. I shouted 'rebels' at them and the crowd simply went wolf-hungry." He smirked for a moment and then continued. "And it was I who told Gig about you and his wife. I have been spying on you and Mrs. More. I had sworn to Gig I would protect his interest and..."

"I understand," I said, patting him on the back. "You had to do what you had to do."

Just then the bush rustled. I flashed the torch in the direction of the noise. There was Gig standing as if he were Lazarus, asked to walk out of the tomb. His gun was pointed in our direction. I could see the shattered shoulder where my bullet had done its damage. He cocked his gun. He ordered me to point the torch first towards myself and then toward the frail man.

"Ah, so it's you two," he breathed. "Socrates, where are my diamonds? Hand them over to me, and I'll let you go."

He asked me to point the torch toward myself again.

"Mr. Traitor, I'm not sure you'll fuck another man's woman so soon. You'd have to wait until after judgment day. How would you like this right between your legs?"

My throat went dry.

I felt a tremendous jolt and a split second later, I heard the bullet explode out of Gig's weapon.

My head crashed on a rock, and I was flat on my back. The frail man rolled away from me as he thudded on the ground. He had saved my life and had been shot instead of me. I quickly reached for my gun and fired six bullets into Gig's stomach. It was the second time I'd used a gun, and both times I'd used it on the same person. He was dead before he reached the ground. I turned to Socrates and cupped his head in my palms.

"You are going to be okay, Socrates. I'm going to take you to an emergency unit."

"It doesn't matter anymore, Badamaci. I just have to tell you one more thing, before I—before—I…"

I interrupted him. I knew what he was trying to say. "You are going to be fine," I said.

"You ought to be thanking your stars, Badamaci," he said.

"Thank you, but why is that?"

"The two big fellows were supposed to kill you just after the rebels stormed Freetown. I saw them threatening Mrs. More to tell them where you were."

Just then he gasped, and spat his life into my hands.

I thought about the diamonds somewhere whose whereabouts were forever locked in the head of the corpse of the frail man. Soon, I remembered that Mrs. Gimi More knew something about them. I recalled the plans she had for the two of us. I picked up the torch and began to retrace my way to Mammy Felleh Cookery shop.

I looked among the corpses, but I didn't find her. As I began to leave the scene, I heard her familiar cry under a fallen tree. I dashed toward the painful sound, and there she was. I urged her to approach as I raised the torch, but under the tree, couched in the agony of double mutilation, she lay sprawled with the blood of rape all over her. Beside her, were the shattered pieces of her husband's coffee mug...

Karamoh Kabba

"HALF A POT FULL"

Her name is Yei Fomba, but she is commonly known as Dabuteh, which is a sobriquet from her father, a humorous man who is fond of calling his children by nicknames he gives to them according to their character or temperament. As a little girl, she was known for her joyous disposition when her mother's cooking pot used to be more than half-full of rice, and thus, the name 'Dabuteh', meaning half a pot full. 'Half a pot full' was an indication that there will be sufficient food for everyone on a given day. But those were the only days Dabuteh enjoyed true humanity in the household of her parents.

Dabuteh was born in a family of over forty children of which nine are siblings from the same mother. But she calls her father's remaining seven wives 'mother' and they all treat her as such without qualms. Her mother had lost a child at birth, whose twin sister died of chicken-pox two years later. But her mother had told her that her twin had called her in the heavens and that was that. Of her six siblings, a boy and five girls, five were sent to school to learn the white man's language. Her eldest sister had married and gone away to a distant land. She was the only one left to help her mother with domestic work and petty trading that helped pay school fees for her school-going siblings.

She lived in a town called Gbamendo in a big compound, situated along the main motor road to a prosperous trading town called Kwendu. At thirteen, she was ready for initiation into the *Bondo* Society. Most of her sisters are recent or old *Bondo* initiates, a ritual that marked their rite of passage into womanhood. Between the ages of ten and thirteen is usually the prime time for *Bondo* initiation ceremony. It was her turn for the ritual. But her father was waiting for a man who would shoulder the expenses, a man who would ultimately become her husband.

Men who are ready for new wives often earmarked their brides at such a tender age. Although she was a beautiful little girl, she had a hard time attracting a prospective husband. Normally, a man would have earmarked her by now, in her so-called prime. Her father encouraged her to dress like a young woman who was ready for the *Bondo* ritual and a husband. She ran around the compound bare-chested, with her virgin breasts exposed. She wore beads of various colours and shapes around her neck and waist. Instead of the ordinary underwear, her mother bought a new *lappa* for her which she now wrapped around the lower part of her body, covering her waist to her ankles. She constantly knotted and unknotted it, flashing her new underwear at putative bachelors, men who were poised for new brides or those who could choose a bride in a split of a second. Her mother regularly treated her to the best corn-roll braids. She also insisted on neatness. Sometimes, she reminded her that "no man wants a dirty woman."

It was a bright dry season *Juma* (Friday) and everything was rosé: the tropical sun was right overhead; the rice farms were ready for harvest; the seasonal fruits were ripe; banana

94

leaves were defoliating exposing ripe bananas from their stems. Altogether, food was in plentiful. The women stood outside in the sun to watch their shadows. They knew it was midday when their shadows appeared beneath their feet – an appropriate time to catch Tilapias and Bullfrogs in their repose. Young women like Dabuteh were glad that they could follow the older women to fish; in the process they learned the art of fishing to make delectable fresh-water fish soup for their future husbands. The older women were filled with excitement that fresh fish and bullfrogs would be part of the diet for their husbands in the evening. They moved helter-skelter to look for their fishing nets and baskets.

Dabuteh had fastened her little fishing basket onto her head-tie and part of the oval wooden frame of her little fishing net under her armpit. She came close to her father and said in a subtle voice: "Father, I am going fishing with my mothers," mesmerized by the presence of two men who were talking to him. They were adorned in huge white gowns and headscarves – looking like ghosts. Her father was also dressed in his *Juma* prayer gown, ready to go to the local mosque for prayers. This is the only time he could be found home, or else, he would be on his farm.

The men had stopped in front of their compound to perform *Juma* prayers before proceeding on their long journey home.
 "Fetch some water for *Kai* (Mr) Alhaji," her father commanded with an unusual show of authority intended to impress his strangers.
"But father, my mothers are leaving me behind," she answered.

95

"Do as I say! And besides, you are not going anywhere today," her father stated firmly.

In a sombre mood, she turned round with her head buried in her chest, biting on the beads around her neck and fetched water for the strangers.

"Dabuteh!" Her father shouted again.

"*Naamu* (Yes Sir) father!" she answered from her mother's room where she had laid down and buried her face on a pillow, weeping in disappointment for being deprived of going fishing. She wiped her face to conceal traces of disappointment before she came running. She stood arms akimbo with her virgin nipples pointing straight at the strangers and waited for whatever further instructions her father might have.

"Go and tell Bondu Dahai, the youngest of my wives, that I have strangers. Help her prepare some food for the strangers. When you are done, wait here... I am going to the mosque with *Kai* Alhaji and I will be back soon." Her father explained.

Whatever her father had discussed with Alhaji was unknown to her, but Alhaji kept stopping by the house each time he went to Kwendu. He brought with him many gifts, ranging from clothes, food and money. Besides the merchandise Alhaji bought at Kwendu, he was a diamond trader who had amassed considerable wealth. It was not a surprise when her parents started arrangements for her initiation into the *Bondo* society. It turned out to be the grandest *Bondo* celebration ever held in the township of Gbamendo and its surrounding towns and villages. Alhaji hired the most famous balladeers from far away chiefdoms to celebrate the momentous occasion. He brought cows, goats and sheep to be slaughtered.

96

"I have not seen so many animals bound for the abattoir for celebrating a rite of passage," an old lady told the *Soko* (Bondo Priestess) gleefully.

The initiation rite to join the sacred society began with her mother. She rubbed on young Dabuteh white clay dissolved in cold water. The poor girl endured the chill of the harmattan winds, compounded by the cold water laden clay. Her mother ministered to her to stay calm and not frit away for the eternal shame of the family. Older women joined the rite by beckoning her and the other would-be-initiates to answer the *Bondo* cry: *Ooooohooo! Ooooohooo*! They snarled, crawled at the putative initiates and prompted them to repeat the *Bondo* cry: "*Ooooohooo! Ooooohooo!*"... No sooner had they repeated the Bondo cry than Dabuteh and the girls matched to the *Bondo Bush* resplendent and arraigned for the initiation to be marked by the memorable merrymaking and feasting.

"You are a woman now," her mother said. "Six moons had gone by since the *Bondo* initiation ceremony and you must be perfectly well now," she continued.
"Yes mum, I don't feel pain anymore," she confirmed her mother's assumption.
"Today, we are going to escort you to your husband at Temasadu," her mother said.
The older women of Gbamendo were delighted to be part of the convoy to accompany her to Temasadu. The marriage ceremony which had followed the *Bondo* initiation six months later was also a topic of gossip in Gbamendo. Every mother wished such good luck for her daughter. Many of them encouraged their children to dress like Dabuteh. In fact, a mother yelled at a lad who came by to

see her daughter, "She is not in a hurry to marry. Don't
come back here anymore."

It became a renaissance time for neatness and cleanliness
for young women in their prime.

"Kumba!" another mother called her daughter aloud. "Go
take a bath and come back for a corn-roll braid," she
instructed.

Before Dabuteh arrived at Temasadu, she did not have a
clue about the cultural differences that surfaced in the forty-
kilometre distance from Gbamendo to Temasadu. Alhaji's
six wives were happy to have a young mate. The youngest
of them who was especially happy said, "Welcome... I will
show you around. If you have any question about the
cooking utensils, let me know. All of them are yours now."

The eldest wife also held her own separate orientation
meeting with Dabuteh: "Here, we wake up at dawn for
prayers. We pray three times during the day and once at
night. Tomorrow, I will give you your *Hijab* (veil), ablution
kettle, a prayer mat and prayer beads. You will also start
taking classes at the *madrassa* next week."

Before she adjusted to the tradition, everything she did
looked bad in the eyes of her mates who had abandoned
their religion, tradition and culture under similar pressure,
when they became married to Alhaji.

Dabuteh was now called Isata Kallay. Islam was not new to
her, but practicing it was very strange. Her father is the first
Islamic convert in her family, but does not demand that his
family practise the religion. He is a *Pommassu*, a supreme
leader of the *Poro* secret society for men, who went back
and forth between his role in the traditional secret society
and the newly adopted religion.

Isata Kallay did the laundry and ironing, she cooked and served food, she bathed her mates' many little children and she dressed them and prepared them for school and *madrassa*. She gave birth to many children. She always had a new born and a toddler to care of at the same time. Her knack to toss herself between housework and childcare was almost like magic. She balanced a two-foot-water bucket on her head, a child on her back and fresh vegetables she picked from the garden in her hands. She ran away several times to Gbamendo for various maltreatments. But her parents always encouraged her to return, "A humble wife shall become blessed with successful children," her father had always said. Sometimes, her father actually took her back to Temasadu when she ran away. To encourage her to stay in the marriage, her father asked her younger sister to live with her and help her with the endless domestic work. They both not only worked very hard, but were sometimes beaten by Alhaji's other wives when certain things were not done properly. Like on one awful afternoon when a piece of charcoal fell on her mate's gown and burnt it as she was ironing the laundry. She concealed the burnt side of the gown to postpone the dreaded confrontation for another day, which she knew would inevitably come. But unfortunately, the mate wanted to use the gown that day to a wedding she had been invited.

"Allahu Akhbar," (God is great) she screamed when she noticed the burn. "Did you burn my gown?" she asked.

"Yes, I did it accidentally," she admitted.

The mate grabbed her by her *Hijab* and dragged her on the ironing table. She forced her head on the hot iron. Luckily for her, the *Hijab* which had trapped between the hot iron and her face protected her against direct contact with the hot iron. But the mate went on, "Don't you realize that my gown is worth more than anything you have ever possessed? You deserve to be burnt in punishment," she screamed as she pressed her head on the hot iron. But Isata Kallay's sister came in on time and grabbed the mate by her hair. She pulled her away from Isata Kallay and gave her a severe beating, which led to her eviction from Alhaji's household.

Alhaji was not ready for another wife any time soon to change Isata Kallay's role in the marriage. She could now see why the wives were so happy when she came into the family. In spite of the hardship, she had eleven children by Alhaji, giving birth to a new baby every year. Adding salt to injury, financial hardship took a heavy toll on Alhaji's family. The diamond business went down because Alhaji was not so young and aggressive any longer and his children were not used to working. Many of them had dropped out of school, a situation that had also threatened her children's position. But she was determined to ensure that his children stayed in school. Alhaji leaned more towards the alternative inexpensive means of education at the *madrassa* for his children at the expense of formal western education. But to ensure that her children stayed in school, the petty trading she had learned from her mother came in handy. The problem remained that Alhaji would not let her distil *omole*, a local gin, because of Islamic values. They battled back and forth, but Isata Kallay ended up leaving Temasadu for the town of Koidu where she went about to distil her *omole*.

Although she did not divorce Alhaji, it was obvious that she was on her own to face life. She could not return to Gbamendo. Her early days in Koidu were full of hardship, equal to a human family that had been abandoned in the wilderness. Her hardship doubled. She worked like a jackass – laboured under extended relatives who had settled down and built houses in Koidu. They knew her real name, Yei Fomba, by which they called her. Yei Fomba had left some of her teenage children at Temasadu; they were merely cared for by Alhaji and his large family. She knew she must do everything possible within her power to fetch them before they perished. Her hands were haggard and her face wrinkled and fatigued due to hard labour. She was constantly frowning from hardship and despair, her brow permanently furrowed from fighting and haggling in the local market with other petty traders over petty cash and customers. She became skinny to the bone and she was always dressed in shabby outfits. The gowns were not desirable anymore and the *Hijab* was discarded. She needed to be strong and swift – she moved hither thither in the local market finding deals on nearly-empty stomach from living on meagre food. But her mind was what remained sharp, as she constantly thought of new ways of overcoming the hardship.

In the end, Isata or Dabuteh overcame the odds. She built herself a house in Koidu. She picked up the rest of her children and settled down. She became the most famous *omole* distiller in Koidu, controlling thirty per cent of the *omole* market in the township. *Omole* retailers came in and out of her house for their supplies. Only then, did Alhaji start to visit her again. Even her mates and their children came to her for help, when it got extremely difficult for them at Temasadu, even though they continued to refer to her *omole* trade as *haram* (sinful). But their presence only reminds her of the cost of the grand *Bondo* initiation

101

ceremony – the long years of struggle and her present achievement in a bitter-sweet mood.

Pede Hollist

BACKHOMEABROAD

The sound of the ringing phone crashed into the woman's sleep. "Damn!" she groaned, reached over the cluttered night stand and felt around for the phone. It seemed only a few minutes since Foday, her husband, kissed her and left to do his paper round. But, in fact, it had been a full two hours. It was now almost five-thirty. She picked up the handset and pulled it toward her head.

"Hello," she growled.

"Caller, please state your name," a computerized-sounding voice instructed.

"Santigie, Ma."

"Will you accept the charges?" the computerized voice continued.

"Yes," the woman snapped, the source of the call jolting her into an irritated consciousness. "Santigie, do you know what time it is?"

"Afternoon, Ma."

"No, it's early morning."

"Good afternoon, Ma. Can I talk to Mr. Foday?"

"He's gone to work."

"Er... er...Miss Claudine, the exchange bureau says I need a code to collect the money."

"I don't have it. Call back tomorrow between eight and nine, America time. Your uncle will have the code for you."

"But. Er...the Alpha jets, Ma. They are bombing the city. Rebels are shooting at people. It took me two hours to get here, Ma." "Use the house phone."

"Not working, Ma. We badly need money. Aunty Liza and her four children now live with us."

"I can't do anything right now. Who is Aunty Liza anyway?"

"She took care of Mr. Foday when he was a baby, Ma."

"Five more mouths to feed? Jesus!" Claudine muttered, took a deep breath, and blew it out slowly, like she was following instructions from a doctor.

Santigie continued. "We have no electricity, no water, not even to wash with. Yesterday, the rebels forced Pa Coker up the street to look as they ... ffff... as they ffff... did it to his wife."

"They raped her?"

"Yes, Ma. Then they make her cook for them. After that, they went to Mr. Bangura's house and took his daughters, Mariangel and Zainab to be their wives. They call it 'Operation Pay Yourself.' "

"My God! What is happening?"

"Lawlessness, Ma. Lawlessness! And now Mr. Sebora has joined them."

"Foday's brother?"

"Yes Ma."

"I don't know what to say. We're praying for all of you," Claudine consoled, suddenly weary. "Call back tomorrow at nine, America time. We'll have the code for you, *ya*."

"Thank you, Ma. Tell Mr. Foday we are praying that Allah will keep him safe."

"Okay. Say hello to your children, Ma. Are they well?"

"Okay, Santigie, goodbye *ya*,"

"I will pray for you as well, Ma because you..."

"Santigie, these collect calls are expensive. Tomorrow, *ya*?" Claudine dumped the phone onto the handset. She rolled onto her back on the bed, pulled the blanket up to her chest, and shut her eyes.

****

"They are different, you know," Claudine's mother had cautioned when she announced she was going to marry Foday.

"Mum, stop talking like this. Foday is an educated man."

"You can take the man out of the bush, but you can't take the bush out of the man. These people…"

"Stop it! Foday is not like whatever you want to say. He has lived in England, and he studied in America. Are you afraid he is going to take a second wife or have his daughters circumcised? Over my dead body! Besides, Foday does not believe in these things."

"When the time comes, he'll not do what makes sense but what they have always done. Don't say I didn't warn you."

"Foday is a good man and will make a good husband and father."

****

Claudine picked up the phone and called her best friend. "You know what pisses me off?" she launched into a rant, "it's Foday!" He does not get that his first obligation is to *us*—his wife and kids. The man has a messiah complex, you know. Feels he has to save everyone."

Claudine pulled off the blanket, sat on the edge of the bed, and ruffled her toes on the carpet.

"You're so right! Living abroad used to mean putting space between us and family back home. Not anymore. Damn phones and e-mail have closed that gap and made them permanent hitch-hikers. Know what happened one morning? I was in the bathroom doing my thing when someone called for Foday, on *my* freaking cell phone. Know what I did? Flushed and hung the mouthpiece over the toilet. Sure did. Have never got a call for him on *my* cell phone since."

105

Claudine stood up, paced up and down the room, phone in hand, her voice edged with urgency.

"All I know is that we can't go on like this. Foday has to face reality. This extended family thing, twenty, thirty people taking a free ride on the backs of one or two people, is crap. It's welfare, plain and simple."

Claudine stood by the bedroom window and parted the curtains. Daylight flooded the room.

"Oh my God! It's almost 7.00a.m. . I have to get the girls ready for school. Talk to you later."

Claudine skipped down the stairs into the kitchen and ran smack into an unsightly heap of unwashed dishes, open drawers and cupboards. Strewn across the kitchen table were yesterday's newspaper, last week's magazines, and used food wrappers. Foday's overalls hung over a dining room chair and a pair of his work boots sat idly in the middle of the kitchen floor. Claudine clasped the sides of her head and shook it. Then she turned around and marched up the stairs to wake her daughters, deciding she would save herself the trouble of preparing lunch boxes by buying breakfast at McDonald's and boxed lunches at the supermarket. She shoved her three girls into the bathroom amid a wail of protests. Relaxed and with time to spare, Claudine deftly handled the morning rituals, simultaneously taking calls for assistance, scrubbing someone's back and buttocks, or brushing somebody's teeth; finding clean underwear, matching odd socks, ironing a dress, combing and adorning the hair on a bobbing head; finding an item for show and tell in school; ensuring that a project is in the right bag; or signing an approval form and at the same time getting herself dressed and writing out a list of "things to do" for Foday. However, this morning the phone call preoccupied

106

Claudine and made her feel vulnerable as she attended to her girls.

"I got it first!" A tussle broke out between the two older girls, eleven and nine, as Claudine washed the youngest, seven, in the tub.

"Na-hun, I did. Mum! Mum! She won't let go of the toothpaste."

"I got it first…."

"Mum. Mum, she is pinching me."

Thwack-thwack! Claudine's wet, soapy hand exploded on the bare backsides of the two girls. Thwack-thwack! Her hand swooped down again, searing the girls' backs with two mopping-up blasts. The strikes had been lightning quick, and savage. The youngest child, who had not been hit and who was still sitting in the tub, started to cry. The bathroom's exhaust fan droned, the older girls wailed in various degrees of bewilderment and pain, and the steam from the hot, running water fogged up the large vanity mirror so that the two targets could not see the reflection of their Mum to glean some reason for their smacks. All they could see was a vaporous shadow floating like one of the ghostly figures of their comic books. Echoing screams, steam, heat, pain, and confusion: the bathroom had become another theatre of operations.

"Shut up! Shut up!" Claudine shouted like an exasperated Mistress at her recalcitrant pupils. "I don't want to hear any crying, *fin!* If I so much as hear a peep from anyone, I'll smack all of you to kingdom come. Do you hear me? Do you? *Fin!*" She smacked her finger against her lips like a clasp on a miser's treasure chest. Their eyes at half mast, the girls swallowed their tears.

The remainder of the preparation for school passed without incident. As she watched her daughters file into the car like soldiers off on a mission, Claudine felt badly that she had hit them. "Let's have breakfast at McDonald's," she announced. Though the shock and sting of the smacking were too new to produce the animated joy an announcement like this usually evoked, it eased the tension in the car. Claudine decided that she would apologise to them when they sat down to eat.

That never happened because when she tried to get a twenty dollar bill from the restaurant's cash-dispensing machine, it showed "Insufficient Funds." She peered at the screen in disbelief and tried for ten dollars: "Insufficient Funds" flashed back defiantly, like a school girl at her enemy for life.

"Damn Foday," she mumbled to herself and bundled the girls out of the restaurant into the car.

"I'm hungry, Mommy. Aren't we going to get pancakes?" the middle daughter queried.

"Shut up! Just shut up!"

****

Foday entered the townhouse around 9.30pm that night and found the home in the same disarray that he had left it in the morning. He grew tense like a tightened bow. He tossed his overcoat onto the couch and marched up the steps. He paused by his daughters' bedroom, looked in, and saw their empty, unmade beds. He strode over to his room. Its bed was also unmade. Worried but angry, he bounded down the steps to the fridge to see if Claudine had left him a note. None! Only his hunger quelled the fury he wanted to unleash. He yanked open the fridge door and scavenged for food. Leftovers everywhere: spaghetti here, macaroni and cheese there, half eaten cups of yogurt, boxes of frozen diet meals, celery sticks, lettuce, cucumbers and carrots. He shoved them aside, looking for the plastic containers he knew would have frozen, weeks-old *plassa*—something green that he could throw in the microwave and gobble up with rice. He had emptied all the compartments of the fridge and the shelves of the freezer before he realised there was nothing that he liked to eat. He seethed like an unmasked spirit. He grabbed a beer, opened it, flicked on the T.V., and flopped on the sofa, his anger at Claudine swelling into rage with each sip of the beer and as he recalled his aunt's words in their phone conversation earlier that morning, when he returned home from his paper round:

"Must we be afraid to call you who we fed, you whose snot we sucked with our mouths, and whose shit we wiped because you are married to one of *them*?" She spoke with the intensity of boiling palm oil.

"Sissy, what are you talking about?" Foday asked.

"Your woman! She did not want Santigie to talk to you this morning. She told him our calls are *expensee*. Who wears the trousers in your house?"

"Sissy, *I do*. I'll let Claudine know that you can call here anytime and that she should treat *all* of you with respect."

"That's what a man should sound like! Now, what happened to the money?"

"I sent it only this morning, but I added two hundred dollars more, to help out. Here's the control number. Oh, okay, give the phone to Santigie…. Yes, I'm fine. You have a pen? Okay, take this down: 919274657. Yes, in your name, Santigie Kamara. Yes, give the phone back to Sissy."

109

The aunt launched another salvo: "Do you know your grandma is sick and that Sebora has gone to join the rebels? You have to talk him." "Sebora is an adult, Sissy. There's nothing I can do about him from here. I'm sorry to hear about grandma, but I have to go now, *ya.* These calls are expensive."

"Expensee, expensee. But never forget family. I am sure your woman does not forget her people. Every day, we pray for you and your children."

"Thank you, Sissy."

"And remember, you are the man in your house."

"Yes, Sissy. I understand."

"And talk to Sebora. Joining these rebels will bring only trouble for us."

"Okay, but I have to go now. Goodbye, *ya*"

"Okay, BAHYAYE."

****

Foday awoke to the noise of activity upstairs and Claudine's voice. He could tell from her tone that she was putting the girls to bed. He jumped up and climbed the first three steps of the staircase, then stopped, turned around, and returned to the sofa, deciding the topics he wanted to discuss with Claudine could not be done amicably or around children. He was not sure which topic to start off with, but he was damn sure that for each he had an array of examples, history, tradition, and common sense that would put to waste whatever counter arguments Claudine offered. So he returned to the sofa and listened for her footsteps on the staircase, ready to pounce on her.

"Why did you take the money I had put aside to pay the mortgage and not tell me? What did you do with it? What sort of behavior is this?" Claudine's questions exploded in quick succession behind Foday's head like concussion grenades. She had lobbed them as she walked toward the kitchen before she appeared in Foday's peripheral vision.

"What?" he jumped, surprised and confused. Claudine stopped in the arch that divided the kitchen from the dining room, and, turret-like, wheeled around and trained her eyes on Foday.

"I went to get some money from the ATM this morning." Claudine was slow, deliberate, and no nonsense. "All the money *I* had saved was gone. *You* must have taken it. Why did you take it, and why didn't you tell me?"

"I needed it." Foday wore a pained, guilty look.

Claudine saw it and immediately felt sorry for Foday-a man with a Master's degree in African History, a former deputy secretary in the Ministry of Education who once lived in a government house and had servants to tend his yard, but was now known at the warehouse of his day job as 'Foday, the African Energiser Bunny' because he always had the energy to work overtime. This her man, was now reduced to stealing from his wife. She looked at him in his overalls, facing cap with the Nike logo, and hobnailed boots, and she saw the struggling man and knew the fight had gone out of her. His rugged look, combined with the scent of cardboard boxes and sweat, intoxicated her. She wanted to have him right there, to take away his pain and give him some of her sweetness.

"Foday, I know you took the money because you needed it, but what did you need it for, and why didn't you tell me?" she coaxed.

111

Foday heard the softer tone and saw her body relax. He pounced. "I wanted my aunt to get more money. I have a responsibility to take care of them, and I'm not going to shirk it."

"What?"

"I said," Foday puffed out his chest. "*I* wanted to send something extra for my folks, so *I* took some money from *our* account. I will put it back on Monday. No one has been hurt by it."

"That's not the point," Claudine snapped, the sexual energy that had been titillating her replaced with the iciness of rejection and indignation. "Let's be clear. *I* put in *all* the money in that account. *You* took it without asking or even telling *me*. And *you* did hurt the kids because this morning *I* could not get any money to buy them breakfast or lunch."

"Cook for them to eat at home and school!"

"Because that's my job and I don't work; because I sit here all day twiddling my fingers and watching television. You take *my* hard earned money so that you can pretend to be Mr. rich-man-in-America to your one thousand and one relatives?"

"Take that back!" Foday barked, his eyes bulging from their sockets. "Family doesn't mean just you and the kids. I grew up in a large household. We shared what little we had. One man's blessings were everybody's blessings."

"Well, the girls and I are getting only your curses and all your blessings are going back home."

"So you're blaming me because I have a large family? I'm not responsible for that."

"That's it! Lack of responsibility, marrying ten wives and having twenty children as if there's no tomorrow. Now *my* kids suffer because your father could not buckle his belt."

112

Foday strode over and stood in front of Claudine. "Don't *ever* talk about my father like that again," he wagged his finger in her face.

"Or what!" Claudine brushed his finger aside and hissed "You want to hit me? Go ahead. That's how you *Salone* men behave when a woman stands up to you. But make sure you kill me, because if you don't, *I* will make sure your ass goes to jail. Maybe, you forget this is not *Salone*. Move out of my way, *daddy do*!"

Foday refused. "This is what Sissy is talking about," he began, though in a less combative tone. "You talk about my people and my father as if you are better than them. You were rude to Santigie when he called this morning. You kept telling him that the phone call was expensive. Is money the only thing that matters to you?"

"Yes, I did say the call was expensive. I hear you tell them the same thing. Why shouldn't I, especially when I can't do anything from here? And Santigie is an ungrateful liar if he said I was rude to him. Now, let me pass." Foday refused to budge. Claudine turned around and climbed the staircase.

"I know why you have this attitude," Foday shouted as she began climbing the steps. "It's because your relatives don't call and ask for money. But we know why, don't we? We know how your father got his money, don't we?"

Claudine stopped halfway up the staircase and turned, her face flushed with anger for the first time. "Don't bring my father into this."

"Why not! Weren't you just talking about my father's belt buckle? What's good for the goose should be good for the gander. Tell me, how did a civil servant get to build three houses, send two children to school in England, and drive a Mercedes Benz on the money he was paid? Cat got your tongue? I'll tell you how. He stole government money, the

113

people's money that should have been used to build roads, schools, and hospitals to help poor, rural folks like my aunts. So if *your* kids go without one meal, they are making up for what their grandfather took away from poor folks."

"Look, my father served *Salone* for over twenty years, helping to build the very schools and hospitals your poor folks are now burning down! Just make sure my money is in the account by morning." Claudine walked up the rest of the staircase and never looked back. Foday heard their bedroom door slam.

****

Their neighbours, a white, middle-aged childless couple, heard the screaming, the angry voices, and the slamming doors. They saw the hurried walks and the furrowed faces coming and going. But for them it was just those Africans being Africans. They could not tell a domestic spat from a party; both involved loud voices, slamming doors, and much coming and going. However, this discord was no party; it was sending the home into slow disrepair. They had bought the townhome with their own money, refusing financial help from Claudine's parents because, Foday said, "we have to be independent." But now they were struggling to maintain it. The downstairs toilet was broken, and they could not spare the money to fix it. Instead, Claudine had warned the girls not to use it. But the youngest forgot when she had to pee. She remembered her mum's injunction just as the water flowed over the seat onto the floor. Recalling the fate of her sisters a few days before, she bolted from the bathroom, determined, if asked, to deny being the cause of the flooding. But she escaped interrogation because Claudine, avoiding anything that might break the undeclared

114

truce with Foday, wiped the floor and taped the seat covers to the basin. So the toilet remained unfixed, like the loose tiles on the roof, the knobs of the children's bedroom door and drawers, the choked garbage disposal, the peeling wall paint, and the broken light and fan fixtures throughout the home.

For almost one week following their quarrel, Claudine refused to cook, so for dinner Foday ate packets of jerk and Kentucky fried chicken and boxes of Chinese fried or Jamaican curried rice. He would come home, push aside the newspapers, magazines, and the previous night's packets of dried up chicken bones, nestle on the sofa, and flick on the TV to watch sports television. After a hearty cholesterol-laden feast, he would drink a beer, go up to his room, and sleep on his own side of the bed, his back to Claudine's back. A couple of times he fell asleep on the sofa and did not wake up until it was time to do his paper round.

One night, he was awakened by piercing pains in his crotch. A string of ants, drunk on grease, salt, and dried up chicken left lying on his lap, had wandered into his trousers. One or two of the ants had stung the flesh of his crotch, in a probing sort of way. These early stings sent the sleeping man's hand down to investigate. Trapped and in mortal danger from Foday's searching hands, the ants lashed out at the surrounding flesh. Foday woke up, jumping and dancing, his crotch alive like a crackling Harmattan fire. He unbelted his trousers, pulled down his boxers, and proceeded to pulverise the ants, one-by-one. It was a satisfying kill.

****

A week of tension had left Foday weary but angry at everyone: Claudine, Santigie, his dead father, Sissy, and his aunts, uncles, nieces, and nephews. Most of all, he blamed Major Kakatua who had dared to author the epic war now consuming his native land when he could not even write a rhyming couplet. Foday had no extra money to stop by the local bar for a draft with some of his co-workers or even to pick up a six-pack to drink at home. Worse, he finished work much too late to stop by one of his friend's house and to drink some free beer. So he cursed Major Kakatua's ancestors and progeny, and planned to lead an Entebbe-style commando raid to rescue his beloved country from the yoke of this upstart and his band of cutthroats. He himself would finish off this thug: a single bullet between the eyes. Or maybe he would do something that had the ring of poetic justice: disembowel him in public view under Freetown's Cotton Tree. Then he would show the onlookers the white cancerous tissue that had eaten up fifty percent of the major's gut. The people would nod their heads. Now they understood why this man had thrown the nation into so much turmoil. He was sick inside. Some would feel sorry for the Major. They would say he too, was a victim, of fate, colonialism, imperialism, and globalization. Still, others would dismiss these views and urge that they cut him up into one thousand small pieces and feed him to the vultures, for they had heard the rebels protected themselves from harm with powerful medicines. Many would still remain mystified, confused, and they'd ask: "Was all the mayhem part of a divine plan for their country?"

But while Major Kakatua and back home were Foday's out-of-the-house and at-work imaginings, Claudine was no fiction in his head whose demise he could conjure up and execute without consequence. She was a physical reality, evident in the arrangement of their furniture, reflected in the bold colors of their home's peeling interior wall paint, and certainly central to their home, for her portrait with the watchful look, hanging midway on the staircase wall, seemed to follow Foday as he climbed up to their bedroom one night, two weeks after their blowout.

Indeed, as he walked into the dark bedroom, the outline of Claudine's outstretched form asserted itself. Her white man's hair, which he loved, fell in loose tresses down her back. Her buttocks protruded through the sheets with inviting defiance. Claudine, smelling the cardboard boxes and work sweat, moved and breathed ever so slightly, just enough for Foday to know she was not asleep.

Attraction. Repulsion. Invitation. Thought-words, sotto voce.

Cardboard boxes. Sweat.
Almond butter with a hint of Jasmine and Palma Rosa.
Warm, sweet, dark.
Tension and heat.
Give!
Have!
Give or I take.
Take for I give.
Mine, yours, ours.
Engorgement.
Exploding contractions.
"Hmmm….Hmmm, Major Kakatuaaaaa!"
"Aaah, aahh, Kakatuaaaaa!"
Operation Pay Yourself?
BackHomeAbroad.

James Barnard Taylor

REMOVING THE VEIL

It was late afternoon and the fierce heat of the sun was finally dying down. As the drumming intensified, the priest sucked at the woman's breast. This was the start of a common curative ritual performed by a traditional healer in the tiny West African village of Bonkehun.

Situated about ten kilometers from the nearest town with paramedical facilities, the one hundred villagers depended on traditional medicines, beliefs and healers. Modern religion and hygiene were not part of their life. Many villagers had died needlessly from treatable diseases like hernia simply out of ignorance. Yani had been married for about ten years now and had given birth to three boys, all of whom had died before their first birthdays. Tamu, her husband, had been puzzled by these deaths. He believed some evil force was attacking Yani's children. He had four girls by the other two wives, Bati and Muna, but Yani, his first wife, was his favourite as she only seemed capable of producing boys. He was determined to put an end to these deaths.

Bonkehun village was very popular for black magic. Its traditional priests were well known and respected for their spiritual powers. After consultations with the elders, Tamu hired the service of a traditional priest to find out the reason of his wife's misfortune. She would then receive healing and protection for her future children. Tamu was a six foot

118

three gorilla of a man who towered above his wives and gave them physical protection as a hen covers her chicks. His ebony skin shone like a newly polished board.

Yani was very polite and hardworking; her beauty shone like a gem in the sun. Fascinated by her small frame and mulatto skin, the product of a relationship between a Lebanese trader and an African woman, Tamu had not hesitated to pay the bride price. Several years later, Tamu, who owned a sizeable farm, had decided to marry Bati and Muna, two years apart so that more hands would be available to farm his plots.

In contrast to the first wife, Bati and Muna were very strong and tall women, each about six feet tall. Bati, who was about two inches taller than Muna, had broad shoulders and big hips, while Muna had slender features. Whenever Tamu was in a good mood, he would slap Bati's hips and pinch her grapefruit sized breasts. They would both laugh, though this was never done in the presence of the other two wives. His wives lived competitive lives. If Tamu smiled at Yani, Bati and Muna would expect their own smiles in turn, and so on. Each of them wanted her equal share of whatever Tamu had to offer. Still, Tamu was not a happy man because Yani's children have died. He had invited the priest to find a cure to Yani's mishaps, and that had cost him two of his prized cows and six chickens.

Yani now lay almost naked on the ground with both breasts exposed and her eyes closed as the priest continued the ceremony. The priest's bloodshot eyes glanced around as he bent down again to suck more breast milk from Yani. She groaned and moaned as the priest sucked from one breast

119

to another like a hungry child. She still had full breasts like a suckling mother even after the death of her last child. The other wives looked on; heads bent in apparent sorrow and show of support for her as the small crowd of the priest's attendants hummed the mournful tune.

The priest suddenly stood up with his mouth full of milk he had obtained from Yani's aching breast and beckoned to the husband to bring a cup. Tamu disappeared inside the hut and reappeared almost immediately, holding a small tin which he used as a drinking cup. The priest emptied his mouthful into the tin and called for some water that he poured into the tin halfway up. He then took a straw from a nearby broom lying on the ground and stirred the concoction. Yani lay motionless on the ground, tired from the ordeal. The priest beckoned to the other wives, Bati and Muna, to stand up and come closer to him. By now a low fire was burning in the compound as dusk was taking hold. The wives stood up, and as the drumming reached a frenzied pitch, the priest handed over the tin to them to drink in turns. Taking part in the ceremony was supposed to prove the innocence or guilt of Yani's mates in the death of her own children. Refusal to drink would mean acceptance of guilt and immediate divorce or even death. Both drank reluctantly...

The priest had also come with his small snake, which he called *"Pekin Bullo,"* to perform the cleansing of Yani's womb. Yani was then carried into the house. Only the immediate family members were allowed into the hut for this part of the ceremony. Yani lay naked on the mat. The priest lit a small stick, which smelled like incense and chanted a few songs. He waved his hands in the air as if appealing to something imaginary to come to him. It was at this point that *"Pekin Bullo"* emerged from the pocket of thick country cloth half-gown the priest was wearing. It fell on the ground, few inches away from Yani, who eyed it suspiciously, pulling her legs together as it crawled closer to her.

Tamu was closely observing everything that what was going on. The priest picked up the serpent and pulled Yani's legs apart. She yielded and her legs were separated like a well-oiled metal door opening noiselessly. Chanting softly, the priest put the creature on Yani's left leg, then the right leg and rolled it up and down. Suddenly, he put it between her legs and coaxed it up into her vagina. Tamu's eyes widened and they seemed to pop out in surprise as the ceremony progressed. He hadn't the faintest idea that the ceremony would include this part when he contacted the priest. Did it matter anyway? He liked Yani very much and would have done anything humanly possible to help her.

Yani was now sweating profusely out of anxiety. The other two wives watched on in disbelief and thanked the gods that their own children were alive and that they wouldn't have to go through the same ordeal. Tamu bit his lower lip as he watched. The snake went a few inches in and not finding an open passage as expected, rushed out. It was as if it had met a closed gate and could proceed no further. The priest picked up the creature, put it in his country cloth, and stood up.

"This has done the cleansing. Her womb is now cleansed, and she will be able to see her children to adulthood," he assured Tamu. "She will also continue to give you male children."

The cleansing of the womb lasted only ten minutes. The priest then took a small calabash full of some green, slimy liquid, cut small crevices on Yani's hips and crotch with a crude knife, and poured the liquid therein, rubbing it in softly but firmly. This was meant to drive the demons away from her flesh and consecrate her waist parts. The cuts had not been deep and the liquid had soothed the wound. Yani didn't even mutter.

After the priest had left, Tamu addressed his other two wives. "We have all seen what Yani has gone through. It could have been any of you. I appreciate your support for her and hope that you will continue to live like sisters," he pleaded. Bati and Muna nodded in agreement. Being unlettered and not exposed to the complex world outside their immediate village community, their simple minds could not disagree with what the priest had done. They had accepted everything like gospel truth.

Five years later

"Leave the dog alone, Falo!" Yani shouted from one corner of the compound, where she sat observing her four-year old boy jumping from one mischief to another. He had just come from breaking a flowerpot, and now he was chasing the dog in circles. She smiled as Falo shook his head in defiance.

"If I get hold of you, you'll be sorry!" she threatened, knowing too well that she could not bring herself to beat him. After losing three children in a row, she had protected Falo like an endangered species. She would not inflict any pain on him, fearing he would fall sick, and God forbid, she would not want to lose him. She had conceived and given birth to Falo a year after the ceremony. Just at that time, a group of health workers had come to the village as part of a sensitization program in general health care, pre-natal, and childcare techniques. Yani had been nominated by the elders as part of a dozen women from the village to participate in the training program. She had learned a lot and her knowledge of hygiene had improved.

"You are now a doctor," her husband told her one day. At the end of the programme, Yani was employed as a nursing aid in the local health center which was set up. She now made sure that her entire household improved their hygiene standards. Cases of sickness decreased in the village, and children stopped dying at the alarming rate that was evident before the health workers came. One evening as they sat down to eat; Yani suggested that her husband wash his hands properly as he had just come from the farm.

"Yes Doctor, but you know I always do," he replied, and they all laughed. The house was now cleaner, and the general health condition of the other wives and their children had improved. Falo was very healthy. His brown skin and curly hair was the envy of many. His mother had seen to it that he took all his vaccinations and medicines on schedule. She bathed him and changed his clothes regularly, and the other wives complied with the strict clinical discipline in the house and compound.

"Maybe if I had been exposed to these health care practices earlier on, my children would not have died. Look at how Falo is growing up. My other children would have grown up like this, healthy and sound," she pondered. "Or maybe it was the priest who helped me so that Falo would not die."

But the more she thought about it, the more she became convinced that the health care training and improvement in hygiene had helped her instead of the spiritual cleansing that she had been put through. She got up from where she was sitting and went into her room. She was tired and needed to rest. Bati and Muna were pounding some corn for the next day's meal. They were lucky as they still had their four children between them. A couple of weeks ago in the middle of the rainy season, all four children had fallen ill in turns, with swollen stomachs and frequent stools. Yani's new knowledge of health and hygiene and the medical care at the local health center had helped the children to survive. Yani felt grateful to the World Health Organization (WHO) health workers who had organized the training workshop, where she had learned a lot and been able to use it for the benefit of her household and community. As a result, things were different, and sickness was not as prevalent as before.

"Don't put it in again!" A voice screamed. Bati and Muna turned. It was Yani standing at the entrance of the hut. Yani, though very tired could not sleep. She had realised that Falo was still outside, and went to see what he was doing. It was at this point that she saw Muna scooping some fallen cornflower from the ground, intending to put it again into the mortar to pound.

"This is why we fall sick. If I had not seen you, you would have put it into the mortar. Please let's try to improve our hygiene standards," she advised. The two women stopped pounding and looked at Yani. They had great respect for her.

"Please listen to the doctor."

They turned towards the voice. It was Tamu who had just entered the compound. He had stood half-hidden among

124

the thatched fence and observed the encounter. They all laughed as he walked towards them and embraced them, one after the other.

Brian James

THE DARK MAN

My father will come for me. I know it in my head, but my heart does not agree; it is beating harder than I have ever felt it beat before. I don't understand why it's beating so hard because I am not afraid. My father will come for me.

On my left a boy about my age looks very much afraid. His name is Sunna. He told me so. I do not think his parents will be coming for him. From the looks of it, he doesn't know either. Also on my left is Sunna's sister, who is slightly younger than we both are. She is crying softly. Her sniffing breaks the silence of the small, candle lit room we are locked in. I wish she wouldn't cry. It makes me feel like crying too, and my father would be angry if he knew I was crying. I have tried to make Sunna and his sister feel better. I have told them that when my father comes for me, they will be free as well. It has done no good. That's because they don't know my father.

Suddenly, the door creaks open. A thin, stooped old man enters. He grins at us. The teeth displayed on his black gums are few.
"The hour has come," he says.
Two men come into the room and force us out through the doorway. One of them pushes me violently. I glare at him. He will be the first one my father handles when he comes. I wonder why my father has taken so long. It has been three days... He should have been here by now.

126

Three days ago, I got separated from my stepmother in a crowded market. My father was away at a meeting in another district. I hadn't wanted to go to the market. I did not want to spend my holiday in the village after a hard term of school in Freetown. I would rather have gone swimming with my friends, but she had made me go with her. I don't really know when it happened. It could have been when I went some way off to stare at a funny looking old man, or when I stopped to tie my shoelace. Either way, I suddenly realized that I was alone and surrounded by faces I didn't know.

I was not frightened at first. I concentrated on finding our red SUV. Hours later I had still not found it, and the sky had started to change. Even then I was not scared. I was just hungry. By myself, I did not know how to get to the place we were staying so I just sat out on the main road and waited. Someone was bound to come looking for me. As I sat on the roadside, a man walked by. He was tall and very dark with tribal marks down the side of his face. For a few seconds he stared at me. I stared back. He looked somehow familiar, but it was only after he was gone that I remembered where I'd seen him before, or if I really knew him at all. It was when darkness began to fall that I started getting concerned. The town did not look very friendly at night. I was beginning to wonder if I should try finding my way home myself when two older boys came by and saw me standing there.

"Why are you standing there like that?" One of them asked.

"Can't you see his clothes? He is one of the *J.C.s*... Are you a *J.C.*?"

127

"I haven't just come from abroad," I answered. "I live in Freetown, and I'm lost."

"How did you manage to get lost?" asked the first boy. "It's your kind that the hunters are always looking for."

I didn't like the sound of 'hunters,' but I said nothing.

"You should come home with us and spend the night there. Tomorrow morning you can look for your parents."

My father had always told me never to follow people I did not know, and I did not want to go with these boys. I also did not want to continue standing on the dark road with all those mysterious 'hunters' around, so I went with them.

"Home" was not what I expected. It consisted of about three or four dusty steps in front of a shop that was closed for the night. People were huddled on the steps and talking in low voices.

"Welcome to our palace, Mister J.C.," said the second boy with a smile. They found us a small space amongst the bodies and we settled down. They produced a piece of stale bread for me; it tasted very bad, but as I was hungry, I ate all of it

"So who are your parents?" they asked me.

"My stepmother has a shop, and my father is an important politician."

They exchanged brief glances and then asked me other questions. We talked for a long time. They told me what it was like living on the streets and the how they got up to each day to find food. I concluded that they were just petty thieves who risked their lives on a daily basis to get food. In this town, the boys told me, if a thief got caught, he was beaten to death. It had never occurred to me how difficult it could be to find a meal.

Some of the other children joined in our conversation. They told me about the 'hunters'. 'Hunters', they said, were people who wore Balaclavas and carried away children whom they found on the streets. Those children were never seen again. There were many different stories about what the hunters did to the children they caught, but my guess was that no one really knew. I told them that when I got back to Freetown I would tell my father about these 'hunters'. I assured them that my father was going to be president of the country soon and that he would deal with the hunters. We talked late into the night. It felt good not being told when to go to bed.

Eventually we fell asleep. The steps were uncomfortable, but I was tired. It seemed only a few minutes later when someone shook me awake. At first I didn't understand what I was seeing. People were shouting and running helter-skelter in the darkness. The world looked like it had been thrown into our washing machine at home.
"Run! J.C. run!" I heard one of my new friends shout. His voice sounded so frightful and urgent that I stood up and began to run as well. But I was too late. I felt hands grab me and lift me into the air. They threw me into the back of a van and someone approached me with a black bag. Just before he put it over my head, I saw his face which was dark, with tribal gashes down the sides. I wanted to say something, but a voice told me not to make a sound. The voice was very rough and coarse so I obeyed. Then the van drove away.

After a very long and bumpy ride, the van stopped and someone pulled me out. The bag over my head was taken off. I found myself in a drab room filled with other

129

children. I looked around for the man with the tribal marks, but he was gone. Some of the children were younger than I, some older. All of them looked very much afraid. As they spoke softly to each other, I learned that 'hunters' had taken them all from the street. Some had been fooled into thinking that they would be sent to school, while others, like me, had just been picked up.

We were kept in the room for a very long time. Every now and then two of the 'hunters' came into the room and took some children out. They never came back in. I was afraid. I knew that if I remained patient my father would come for me. Even when a day later my father had not arrived and the 'hunters' had come for me and two other children, I still refused to cry. My father is a powerful politician. I knew in my heart that he would not let anything happen to me.

It has been three days now. I am being led through dark bush by the stooped old man. Sunna and his sister are walking behind me. My feet hurt. My father will be coming anytime now. I can almost feel his presence. Presently, we enter a clearing. A large fire burns in the centre. Men stand silently around the fire, naked except for white underpants. Their faces are painted with white stripes. My heart pounds faster because they look so scary. Beside the old man stands the dark man with the tribal marks. He is the only one who is fully dressed. He stares at me. I try hard to think why he looks so familiar but my brain refuses to work. Out of the darkness, a pair of hands grabs me and ties a smelly piece of cloth tightly around my mouth. The same is done to Sunna and his sister. Someone fetches a rope. It is when they start to tie me up that I really begin to feel afraid. Where is my father? Why has he not come to save me? I begin to

130

struggle, but I am easily overpowered. We are led to a mound of dirt. Beside the mound is a large dark pit that looks like a grave. We are lined up in front of the pit. Suddenly, loud drumming starts and the men begin to dance and sing songs that I do not understand. I now realize why Sunna and his sister are so afraid. I try to scream, but I cannot.

At that moment, a big man enters the clearing and walks towards the fire. He is wearing a flowing blue gown. Even before the flames light up his face, I know from his gait that he is my father. My joy knows no bounds. I knew he would come to save me. He would be so proud to know that I did not cry even once. I want to shout for joy, but I cannot open my mouth. I want to jump into his arms and tell him what these evil men have been doing but I can't move.

He strides over to the old man. I wait eagerly for him to release a wave of his terrible temper. Strangely he bends down and whispers something into the old man's ear. He then shakes the tribal man's scarred hand. It is only then that I recognize him. He works at one of my father's factories. My father kneels before the old man. As he does so, our eyes meet. He looks away quickly. I cannot believe what I am seeing. I do not understand. Two other expensively dressed men go to kneel beside him. Their gowns are shaken off and they are left in their underpants. The old man raises his arms and begins to chant. He tells my father and the two men that someone with a scary sounding name is pleased with their valuable sacrifices and promises to grant them power in return.

Sunna suddenly lurches forward and falls into the pit. His sister is pushed after him. There has to be some kind of mistake. Have I been bad? Am I being punished? Can somebody explain this to me? I am pushed in. It is when my feet hit the bottom of the pit that I fully understand what has happened. As the dirt is shovelled over us, the last thing I see is the scarred face of the dark man.

Frederic Borbor James

THEIR SPECIAL DAYS

Their apartment at No.3 Manfred Lane was modern and convenient. It had three bedrooms, the largest of which had a built-in toilet. Five young, enterprising bachelors lived in this apartment: Tamba, Keifa, Teddy, Bondawa and another man they all considered their mock uncle. The master-bedroom was occupied by their mock uncle, the second biggest room by Tamba, who was a co-worker of Keifa, and the third by Keifa, Teddy, and Bondawa.

Their mock uncle was the Chief Bartender at the most prestigious hotel in Gracetown. Each day he returned home from work with large sums of money, some packets of expensive cigarettes and a reasonable quantity of hard liquor. Under his supervision, all the inmates lived like lords.

The men had two servants to attend to their needs and take care of the apartment. These servants were obedient and hard-working young men. In the morning, they would sweep and dust the rooms, clean the toilets, prepare breakfast and launder their clothes every four days. Before going to work, all these privileged men had to do was look in the general wardrobe for some clean and ironed outfit to wear. Their lunch and dinner were prepared by the numerous fiancées and girlfriends that the bachelors had. Collisions between members of these two groups were some of the many dramas that the tenants enjoyed at No.3.

133

Saturday and Sunday were their special days of the week at No.3. They referred to Saturday night as Cowboys' Night and Sunday as the Holy Day. Saturday for them started at 9.00 a.m. with breakfast, followed by two hours of chat on any topic under the sun. Next came a long period of 'boozing', interspersed with light lunch and long and short worship sessions by pairs of worshippers. The latter activity lasted until about 6.00 p.m. when they all retired to their bedrooms for about four hours, so that they can regain energy for resuming the evening session.

The evening session took them to almost all the nightclubs in the city. They had their own 'private car' in which they made these trips. It was a taxi owned by their mock uncle. They would always start with the less outstanding nightclubs and end up at the most sophisticated. On average they spent about twenty minutes in each night club, bar or restaurant. Everywhere they went they replenished their beers, played the jackpot, danced, and then departed.

Sometimes they went in pairs. Bondawa never really went in a pair at any given time. He was always the odd man in the group, and there were all indications that his oddness was an embarrassment to his friends and they were planning to do something about it. Sometimes most of their Holy Days were spent on the 'altar' with the opposite sex, praying to Cupid. It was done in rotation. The female sex came in turns to receive the so called 'Holy Water'.

On one Holy Day, an early worshipper came to the 'altar' in room two. She arrived at 7.00 a.m. to be precise. She had armed herself well enough to arouse the phallic powers of her god. No sooner had she stepped into the parlour after Bondawa had opened the door for her, than the aroma of perfume permeated the whole apartment. She was tall, dark complexioned; her thick shoulder length hair added to her beauty as her lips, which were thin and red. When she smiled, she displayed a perfect set of teeth, with a fine gap in the middle. The looks of this worshipper took Bondawa's breath away. He stood looking at her, dumbfounded.

"I want to talk to Tamba, please," she said.

"Please come and sit down while I look for him," Bondawa instructed, indicating the sofa. She sank into it like a boneless corpus, making sure that her skirt would not rumple.

Bondawa turned the bolt, and to his surprise, the door opened with unusual ease. Roused by the creaking door Tamba raised his head from the bed, the frown on his face giving away his displeasure at the interruption.

"An angel is waiting in the living room to worship with you," Bondawa remarked light-heartedly.

"Please Bondawa, don't spoil my Holy Day. I have not made any bookings with an early worshipper," Tamba said, stretching his limbs and yawning.

"Look, the master room is empty. I will ask her to try *altar* one"

Tamba struggled out of the bed, wrapped himself in his cover cloth, and walked to the door, limping as if he was nurturing an injured leg. When he set eyes on the unexpected visitor, his reaction was indescribable. "Come on in darling," he said, trying to be romantic all of a sudden.

Soon, Reggae hymns filtered in from room two, drowning the several voices that usually greeted the rising sun. It was a sunny day; the living room was already illuminated by the beam from the morning sun. Intermittently there were echoes of 'halleluiah amen', as the worshipers got consumed with the Holy Spirit.

Teddy intruded Bondawa and his guest's company with an anxious look on his face. Bondawa had never seen Teddy look that way. He had always looked excitable, bubbly and humourous.

"What's the matter? Some complaint about Martha"? Bondawa asked…

"Come off that. I can always take care of that woman. It is something else that is worrying me. It concerns my whole future."

"Can we talk about it?"

"Yes, Bondawa, we can. That is why I have joined you," Teddy said, swinging back and forth in his chair.

"Mum."

"It is about my schooling, I'm having a hell of a problem with it. You know how far away we stay from school, with the current transportation problems, I get to school late every day. Coupled with this is the problem of accommodation. There is no convenient place at home for me to sit down and write my notes, do my assignments and study. I want to apply for admission to college next year. "What do you think?"

"If I were you, I would continue until the end of this academic year."

"But, Bondawa, what will I benefit by continuing? Nothing! Seven or so months of working will earn me some money to buy some of the basic things I would need in college."

"You are the one wearing the shoe, Teddy; you know exactly where it hurts you."

Presently, Tamba appears on the scene, walking hand-in-hand with his co-worshipper, both of them beaming with smiles. Meanwhile, a tallish, hefty girl bustling with life, strides stupendously through the main entrance. Without any ceremonies, she walks up to Tamba and embraces him with a compassionate kiss.

"Say boy, I've caught up with you today! You are hardly found in this place. From now until dusk we are going to be together," the new worshiper declared, still holding Tamba in her arms. Tamba stood bewildered, motionless and dumbfounded. He searched his mind for something to tell this buoyant but strange invader. He was a chicken-hearted, lean fellow, not experienced in tackling a problem like this. He was shaking like a mouse facing a cobra, with nowhere to escape.

"But I have no appointment with you. Why do you have to spend the day with me?"

"Come on, darling. You want to refuse me now? What has suddenly gone into your stupid head?" She dragged Tamba along to the bedroom.

Tamba was weak, unable to put up a fight. He looked at Teddy and Bondawa, his eyes imploring them to help. The first worshipper stood helplessly with her eyes moist. She was certainly a well-groomed lady from a respectable background, one who would not put up a fight in a situation such as this. She would prefer to cry until her grief went away. As Tamba was being dragged to the entrance of his own room, the 'aristocratic' girl burst out in spite of herself:

"Please rescue my darling from this monster; he does not love her. Please help!"

She was the actual target. She was only being provoked to talk. Before we could intervene, her dress had been torn off from her slender body and was receiving hot slaps. It was a grotesque spectacle. The victim tried to hide her breasts, unmindful of the blows that were developing blisters in her mouth. We quickly drew the window curtains to obstruct the view of passers-by as it would be inimical for us if a member of the Fannah family (our landlords) were to watch the show or hear about it.

Teddy had taken up employment as a pupil teacher in a primary school close to Bondawa's, also in the afternoon shift. By 11.45 a.m. every Monday through to Friday, they would leave the house together for school and would return home latest 6.30p.m. Teddy and Bondawa discovered that the life style at No.3 was not good for both of them as they had ambitions to further their education. They discovered that it was not good for them to be drunk most of the time when they had to prepare their lesson plans and to read novels, at least two per month, to improve their English. They also discovered that life at No.3 was forcing them to live above their means. They planned to stay aloof from the rest of the group, but it was not easy.

Coming home in the evening after school they often found someone boozing, who would call them to join him. "Hey, teachers, there are some pints of beer here to drink, plenty of it. Why not join me? Life is meant to be lived, when you can; you won't regret it if you should die today or tomorrow," the person would say. So the invincible hands of sensuality engulfed them firmly at No.3.

138

One Friday evening at about 11.00 p.m., Uncle came home from work with a young girl who was extremely beautiful, although some proofs of life's toil and drudgery scarred her physical appearance. She was about five feet six inches tall, slender, and dark with prominent tribal marks on both cheeks. As they entered his room, Uncle called Bondawa and told him: "Bondawa, this is Tonyah. She says she knows you and has been longing to meet and talk with you. The two of you can talk in here until tomorrow morning. No need to hurry at all," he said as he left, locking them in. "Excuse me, do I know you"? Bondawa asked the girl, feeling uncomfortable and embarrassed.

"We will know each other very well tonight, Bondawa. Don't you worry," she answered, eyeing him affectionately. When they had first entered their living room, she looked placid and innocent, like a sheep to the slaughter-house. However, she was soon giddy and coquettish. She lay on the bed and began to roll back and forth, giggling like a child.

"Do you have any idea why he has behaved to us like this, Tonyah?" he inquired.

She got up from the bed, held him by the hand, and said, "Please don't worry, my baby. I love you very dearly, and I am going to keep you very comfortable tonight." She planted a kiss on his right cheek. It was warm. He recoiled and rushed to the door in torment, shook the bolt, but it was locked. He sighed and faced the girl again.

"Jesus, I cannot understand this stupid act. How can Uncle lock me up in a room alone with a girl I've never met before?" he exploded.

"You are simply refusing to understand, but as a grown up you should know why. Your friends are worried that you

139

are not virile and have asked me to come and perform some ceremonies for you," she said with an animated laugh.

"But that is not their business. They have merely brought you here to waste your time. They cannot force me to….."

"You are in for blackmail, so you have to comply."

"What do you mean?"

"They say you are not a man, no matter what claims you make of your manhood. I am here to prove them right or wrong. They are all waiting for my report. You have to prove to me that you are a man, Bondawa, if you certainly are. I am paid to tell them the truth," she said, sounding quite relaxed now.

"I cannot understand this stupid idea at all," he said, pacing the massive room, Tonyah now looking at him sympathetically.

"Please come and sit by me. You don't have to work yourself up like that over an issue such as this. You are attractive; I just don't know what is wrong with you... As he sat down she caressed him gently and her fingers began to explore his body expertly."

"But Tonyah, why did you allow yourself to be used like this?" he asked, beginning to be interested in her.

"Money, Bondawa, money! In Missilah today, a good number of us can do anything for money. It is not our fault, we have to survive," she said, looking away from him. To his surprise, she was weeping softly, her fingers resting numbly on his body. He was so overwhelmed by sympathy that he held her in his arms and kissed her.

She clung to him helplessly and wept freely. He wiped her face, and soon they were being possessed by the Holy Spirit. There were murmurs of hallelujah and amen. When the

Holy Spirit departed from them, they lay on the bed, exhausted, looking at the ceiling.

"Why did you cry, Tonyah?" He broke the silence. She was soon crying all over again, the tears flowing down her cheeks unchecked.

"I have gone through some bitter experiences in life, Bondawa, even at this early age. It is not my intention to be on the street having affairs with every male that can pay me for doing so. It is a painful and dehumanizing business. I do not enjoy it at all, but I cannot do otherwise." She had now stopped crying and was wiping her face with the back of her hand.

"How did it all begin?"

"It is a long story, but I will try to be very brief," she said, looking away from him. "My plight started when I got pregnant in Form Three. My parents drove me from home to join the one who impregnated me. My baby's father did his best to make me happy, but apparently, he was ill-prepared for the task. He and I lived in a very tiny cellar, and our food was always grossly inadequate. In spite of all this, we grew to love and respect each other, and we had a strong desire to survive."

She turned to him suddenly and was now looking piercingly at him. "Our baby showed up a couple of months later. I was only fifteen years old. It was a healthy baby boy, an effigy of his father. We loved and cherished him. The rains were very heavy that year, and food was difficult to come by. Our tiny room was always damp. The poor boy contracted pneumonia and died. I became very aggrieved and wept for two good days without eating. My only desire then was to die, but my baby's father assured me that we

141

could have another one soon, and that it would live." She embraced Bondawa and resumed sobbing uncontrollably.

"You have been a brave girl all along. You don't need to break down now," he said stroking her thick hair. She rose from the bed and began to pace the room thoughtfully.

"After the baby's death, he left me to go in search of fortune in the diamond mine. Two months passed without a word from him. Then three months, four months; I started going out at night to look for money to feed myself. After one year, it became a trade for me. Through this shameless trade of being a sex worker I'm able to feed and clothe myself, but it is a hard life, Bondawa. We are misused and abused each night we go out."

She came back to the bed, opened her handbag, took out a mirror and some cosmetics, re-did her make-up, and was ready to go.

"Sorry that your friends connived with me to corrupt your life. I hope you will forgive me." She went to the door and knocked on it three times. The message got home, the key turned in the lock, and the door was flung open. The girl walked gingerly out of the room into the living room, and there was applause.

When Bondawa went to bed that night, many images invaded his mind: images of numerous unwanted babies lying in dustbins and gutters; images of street children idling in parks, cinema halls, and other entertainment centres; images of disabled people sitting in strategic places in Gracetown begging to survive; images of prison centres full of young criminals; images of young men and women parading the streets of Gracetown frustrated to insanity; images of poverty amidst affluence; images of a huge number of university graduates going in search of job opportunities that did not exist; images of the economic, educational and other vital systems on the verge of collapse; images of a society consumed by corruption and images of Tonyah carrying a dead baby in her arms. Where has it all gone wrong? In his dream, he began to weep for Tonyah and for himself.

Mohamed Combo Kamanda

WASTED TRUST

The rain was pounding the softened earth. The accompanying thunder was equally fierce as was the lightning which lit the merciless sky that appeared to have opened up. It was nothing unusual at this time of year in this part of the world. Although it was already dark and raining hard, the lightning made it possible to discern in the distance a large, lone and uncharacteristic white mansion, surrounded by tall exotic evergreen trees. About a hundred meters from the mansion, a lonely but intimidating hill stood defiantly. At its tip was a forest fragment. Legendary accounts suggest that this forest fragment had been home to the fiercest creatures and mysterious events ever known. One of those creatures, the one-eyed and one-red-tooth *'haniwaa'* - loosely translated from Mende as "the great one", still lingers in the childhood imaginations of the descendants of Golagbaahun, a sprawling village along the highway to the eastern province's notorious diamond mining town of Tongola. On the fringes of the forest a figure, dressed it seemed in a military fatigue, was clawing its way out of the woods. The tall, strongly built and grotesque looking figure was carrying a sniper rifle: one of the cruel and enduring relics of the brutal conflict that had come to characterise this society. Each time, the figure sighed again and again, after slowly bringing her night eye to the viewfinder.

144

A black glittering Mercedes Benz swerved its way into the mansion's driveway at exactly 6.00am. Arrogantly, out of the car stepped a tall, dark looking man, dressed in West African style attire – the *agbada* – a three-piece suit consisting of a flowing gown with embroidery around the collar, a safari top and pair of trousers to match. In the man's company were two ladies, both of them dressed in a pair of Levi jeans and a plain jersey top, and another huge and strongly built man, a bodyguard perhaps?

Presently, the woman in military fatigue on top of the lone hill shifted into a more comfortable position as she eagerly looked down at the mansion and the figures that now filled its front area. She flicked her wet dreadlocks from her forehead and peering at the dial of her wristwatch, she tried to dry it up. After a short while, she focused the rifle on the tall dark man just as the bodyguard inched his way into the mansion, flirting with one of the two women like newly-weds on a honeymoon. The woman in military fatigue growled in anger and threw the weapon on the ground. She snatched up a machine gun; she must have been well armed for this mission. She got up and viciously shot aimlessly at the mansion. As the kissing couple heard the gunshot zipping past, the woman disengaged and scurried into the mansion to safety. One of the men turned fearfully in the direction of the shot's origin, gasping as he recognised a figure in military fatigue that was aiming another round in their direction. He tried to duck but it was too late; three bullets hit his chest. A few seconds after the shot, he fell dramatically, like a log on the cold wet tarmac.

"I hope I haven't caused a stir in the house… how will my boys know that I'm the one shooting to protect them?"

145

Sniper queried. "In any case the mission should have been accomplished by now" she reassured herself.

By now, the morning sun was beginning to surface above the forest's trees. The characteristic morning dew on the hilltop that accompanies tropical downpours had disappeared, so it was possible to notice the *nyangobaa* - the Mende word for eclipse – quite a strange sight at this time of year, except that it was a sign that something strange will happen or would have happened. The eclipse was already beginning to shield the sun and its rays.

The following day, word had already spread that a streak of murders had occurred at Taila's Lodge. Among the dead was Mr. Jongo Taila himself, the enigmatic businessman of Golagbaahun and his womanising cousin. Mr. Jongo Taila was a household name in Golagbahun and beyond. His booming restaurant was a popular resort for drivers of all sorts of commercial vehicles that plied the route to and from the diamond mining eastern region's headquarters, a hotchpotch and metropolitan settlement in the hinterland. Rumours were rife that Taila's sudden rise to fortune was not entirely unconnected with belief in supernatural powers. Part of his enigmatic personality resided not only in his shady deeds: mysterious disappearances of his siblings, peculiar noises that oozed out of his compound during periods of full moons, but also in the supreme power of the guests that regularly frequented his mansion, some of them from as further afield as the fringes of the Sahara! It was common knowledge that Taila's body was fortified against all kinds of evil, including gunshots!

"No bullet will ever pierce his under vest," one of his personal assistants was reported to have said to a bewildered audience.

As well as playing host to the most potent 'juju' men and women, Taila had made numerous trips abroad to renowned destinations for supernatural worship. As a result, reports about the unexpected assassination of an inscrutable, prosperous and awesome son of the soil easily made headlines on the national papers and TV. Safiatu, popularly known as Laama because of her chattiness, presented the news on the national TV:

"The death is reported of Mr. Jongo Taila, renowned proprietor of Ndeigbohmei Enterprises in Golagbahun. Funeral arrangements will be announced later."

The breaking news which was sombre, solemn and heart rendering, was juicy gossip for the village dwellers, notably the petty traders in its local market.

"Have you heard, my sister?" one market woman inquired of another.

"Oh, about Kenawa's flight to heaven?" she remarked sarcastically.

"Did he actually fly as it had been predicted?"

"How can he? I hear he had no chance against Sniper Rifle's gang. He was battered beyond recognition".

"Hmm, ah duniya! So, all this talk about invincibility and die at the time of his choosing were just lies!"

"Let me tell you my sister, you should never trust a word from these money grabbing *krahmohkohs* of our generation. It doesn't matter where they come from: locally or internationally. They are humans, just as us!"

"Who should be trusted?"

It was common knowledge that boastful Kenawa, a firm believer in *kukumeh* - a term commonly used among the natives of Golagbaahun community to refer to magic and wizardry - had predicted that at the time of his death, he would fly into the heavens above and no living mortal would set eyes on him. Such was the influence of this enigmatic man's affluence that it was impossible to question anything you heard about him, particularly if you were subject to the poverty that characterised most households in that part of the country. He was known to play host to the most prominent *kukumeh* experts, local and international alike. Everyone in Golagbaahun knew about the powerful sorcerers and renowned traditional herbalists that had visited Kenawa's Lodge and lived there for months on end, insulating him from harm, danger, and even death! Or, so they thought. One of them, Suwui Taajo, was quoted as saying: "Kenawa will die at a time of his own choosing." Wishful thinking!

Was it not intriguing that the news about this famous man's death was cast by Safiatu, one of his many girlfriends? After the newsflash, Safiatu threw her long wig into shape. It was easy to perceive the solemnity in her voice. As well as dressing up in dark grey suit to signify the tragedy, Safiatu's characteristic jovial demeanour had given way to a gloomy outlook that spoke volumes about her state of mind. After reading the news, Safiatu grasped her bottle of Tutik mineral water, got up and left, bereft of all niceties. She had barely got into her car when Big Joe, another of late Jongo Taila's bodyguards appeared on the scene. Big Joe was generally a man of very few words and a good listener.

"Big Joe!" Safiatu demanded. "Where were you at the time of Kenawa's tragic end?" Kenawa, the big one, was the

148

nickname of Mr. Taila. Big Joe looked sternly at Safiatu, straight into her eyes. After a while, without uttering a word, he calmly took a long drag off his cigarette. Big Joe ignored the question. His personal grief was visible. As Taila's body-guard, the death of his boss had serious implications for Big Joe, not least, that he was the prime suspect, the mastermind of an assassination designed to foully eliminate so as to inherit his master's wealth. On one occasion, Big Joe had been implicated in a forgery scam; he was accused of forging his master's signature on a cheque that could have earned him millions of local currency. He was momentarily incarcerated but later released without charge. So, Safiatu's accusation was not entirely unfounded. It was for a good reason. She grabbed his arm and whispered threateningly:

"If you're behind this, you'll pay for it."

Big Joe looked at Safiatu tearfully, brushed her aside and said, "The truth will out."

****

Mariatu opened her eyes, shaking with terror; her pale skinny hands on her lap. She looked fearfully around the dull room in which she had been confined. There were black drapes across the room's only window. She could hear voices behind the door to her left. The dusty doorknob turned slowly. She noticed the door opening slightly, yet no one entered until after a while. Swiftly but silently, two people crept out of the shadows and gripped her arms tightly. One of them was a well-built female figure dressed in military fatigue, the same fatigue that was worn by the woman who had fired shots at the mansion. Sniper Wolf walked menacingly towards Mariatu, this time, tossing and turning a pistol in her left hand.

"So, tell me!" screeched Sniper Wolf. "Is it true that you have been sleeping with Kenawa? Is it true that you were with him on the night prior to his death?"

Mariatu was too frightened to offer any explanation.

"You very well know that Kenawa was engaged to Laama, the news reporter, didn't you?" she barked, grabbing hold of Mariatu's face with her right manicured fingers... Realising that Mariatu was not offering the desired responses; Sniper Wolf smirked angrily, tearing off Mariatu's face with her finger nails.

"If you don't co-operate with us, you will die and rot in this cell!" she threatened. Sniper Wolf then left the dark room, slamming the door with her left heel.

"What have I done to deserve all this?" Mariatu moaned in agony. How could she have predicted such an end to her one-sided and shameful relationship with Kenawa? How many suitors had her father turned down? In her prime, Mariatu knew she was every man's dream to have, to hold, and to cherish. There she was, locked up in a dark room in the middle of nowhere for a crime she knew nothing about, apart from the fact that she was in the mansion when Kenawa was pronounced dead by the coroner. Memories of her emerald past came flooding back, renewing her old wounds.

Mariatu was the fourth of six children to her mother. Her father, Kaamoh Fodie, a learned Qur'anic teacher, was chief of the Imams in Golagbaahun and its surrounding villages. His reputation rested on the power of his *Kaavaa* – locally made devise used for writing. Everyone in the community knew about Kaamoh Fodie's prowess in using Qur'anic verses for causing evil. Promiscuous young men knew that the price of a love affair with any of his many wives ranged from a vicious snakebite that culminated in paralysis to mysterious, unexplained deaths. Such was the power that Kaamoh Fodie wielded that ordinary people in Golagbaahun could not have courted any of his blissful, beautiful children for matrimony, nor for anything else. How ironical that the daughter of such a skilled and knowledgeable Qur'anic professional could end up at the mercy of a dubious businessman or an evil gunwoman, like Sniper Wolf?

The saying goes that one person's riches derive from the toil and drudgery of thousands. So it seemed was the rise to prominence of Kenawa. From a very humble background, he had been lucky to be handpicked by a white man who had come to serve as a missionary in the local church. Father Nohbehteh, as he came to be popularly known, demonstrated a keen interest in young boys, an interest that still remains a mystery to date. His unique ways and devotedness to the Church had so much endeared him to the poor unsuspecting villagers that parents were reported to have queued up in donating their sons to the priest for grooming them into the Christian faith. Did you say for abusing them? In the end he had a sizeable army of young, talented, handsome boys in his parsonage. Even after his retirement, this white priest maintained contact with the boys, who were now full-grown men, through their leader – Kenawa. Could it be that Kenawa's wealth had been fuelled by exploitation? Rumours were still rife that the priest, now of blessed memory, donated huge sums of money to each of his *heirs,* the boys who had lived with him. It has to be admitted that whether the wealth had been foully acquired, Kenawa had surely put it to very good use. At the time of

151

his death, he had owned a stream of five star hotels, a fleet of very expensive cars, land and other property at home and abroad.

Thinking about it now, Mariatu could still not forgive her father for having forced her into such a relationship. By that time, she was deeply attached to the first love of her life for who she still yearns... Kenawa had promised that he would support her in every way to continue her education, even to a postgraduate degree level! And what has she gained from him, instead? Nothing! Absolutely nothing; apart from food, clothes, the many pairs of shoes and the one bedroom to which she has been literally caged for sensual abuse. She wasn't supposed to leave her bedroom for any reason whatsoever because it was self-contained. If she needed anything, she rang a bell, and a servant had brought it for her promptly. At those times when Kenawa had felt like having intimacy with her, he had slipped into her room past midnight and left before the first cockcrow. So, how was she supposed to know anything about such a man who belonged to others, a man whose affairs still remained a dark mystery to her?

Mariatu, dressed in a nightgown, sat in a corner of the cold, dark and grey room lost in imagination. She thought hard about the events of that fateful night... At about 11.30pm Kenawa was still in a meeting with his business partners, as it appeared. She could tell from the expletives, tone and pitch of the language used that the argument was heated and indecent at worst. That night, there was a huge flurry of activity. Cars moved to and from the mansion, the sound of footsteps or heavy boots could be heard in the background, as if there was a military parade in the heavy downpour. Sometimes, it was all action and no speech.

"Gentlemen, thank you all for coming", the hoarse voice said after clearing his throat. "I have a simple mission for you, Sniper."

"Your wish is our command, sir" Sniper asserted, looking at Gunyon and members of his team.

"Someone needs to be eliminated; he has grown too bigheaded and full of himself."

"Who may I ask?"

"I want to teach everyone a lesson by this example, Sniper" Gunyon said firmly. Gunyon was a boyhood friend of Kenawa; perhaps one of those he grew up with under the auspices of Father Nohbehteh. Relations between the two had deteriorated rapidly after Kenawa recently completed and inaugurated his second 5 star Hotel on Banana Island. It was like the last straw. To execute his plan, Gunyon had recruited Sniper Wolf, a former rebel commander who had distinguished herself for eliminating enemies. She was a marks-woman.

"If you get riches from the earth, don't exempt the sand from it. Someone who has prospered from our sweat: resources that belong to more than five people, now thinks he is more blessed than we all are." Gunyon explained.

Sniper and his gang immediately figured the target Gunyon was referring to; it was his business partner, Kenawa.

"Here is your advance payment, $3,000.00; the rest of your money will be paid after the job is completed."

"What is the time frame for this assignment?" Sniper inquired.

"ASAP; tonight if possible; I understand he is organising a birthday party for one of his concubines at the White House."

"There cannot be a better time", Sniper gloated. "Consider it done, sir."

This meeting between Gunyon, Sniper and his men preceded the night of the thunderstorm that had battered the region. So, before nightfall, even before the rain had started, Sniper, the ugliest woman in town, and her murderous gang had set out on their hideous mission. Her role was to keep watch on the white house and nip any trouble in its bud. The junior members of her gang had to do the dirty job...

And so, all the *kukumeh* paraphernalia located at different parts of Taila's Lodge for dispelling the forces of evil and the angel of death were rendered impotent against the arsenal of Sniper Wolf and her gang. The 'bullet proof vest', protective shield against gunshot, had failed to protect its master.

Here lies the remain of Jongo Taila;
The supreme businessman of Golagbaahun in Mendeilia,
Who trusted juju, instead of God, the ever living Voodoo.
In talismans and medicinal earthen pots his hope and trust resided;
Now in ruins six feet below at his mansion
His remains preside.

Have the human race in Taila's demise been taught a lesson
On greed and blind trust?

Yema Lucilda Hunter

IF EBENEZER COULD TALK

Hmm. These days, all I am is an observer of other people's lives – a bystander- except that I am not even that. I am flat on my back most of the time and incapable of saying anything intelligible. I'm sure that when people see me like this for the first time they think, *Ah, yah! Ben John who used to be so handsome!* Or, with an inward sigh, *Hmm. What is man?* Or even, *I'm sorry for him; but he had it coming.*

I did have it coming – stopping my high blood pressure tablets because that evangelist pronounced me: "Healed by the blood of Jesus!" I wonder whether I would have had the stroke if I had kept really close to God after the crusade; if I had gone to church more often and all that sort of thing. But I am not a religious person, never have been, never will be, though I do believe in a higher power. I only wanted to please Becky, who took me to that crusade. I will do anything to please her; especially after the way she took me back following that unfortunate episode with Adela. Hmm. Will I ever forget the slap she gave me? Who would have thought my pint-sized Becky was strong enough to land such a blow?
Adela Williams.
"Ebenezer, what came over you?"
Anyway, it was my own fault that I ended up like this. Becky always warned me about my temper and for a good reason, as it turned out. I know I should have kept my cool

155

when Pa Alimamy came to tell me that thieves had broken into the store yet again and had taken ten bags of cement and many of the iron rods I bought to build a house for Becky's brother. Instead of keeping my cool, I lost my temper in a big way. I blew a *gasket*, so to speak. Bad words erupted from my mouth like compressed steam in front of my grand-daughter, Linnie, scaring the poor child out of her wits so badly that she burst out crying. Becky came running, just as I felt something like a hammer blow to my head. The last thing I remember clearly is her crying out, "Pa Alimamy, don't let him fall!"

And here I am, silenced, perhaps for good; it seems, with only one working arm and one working leg. I just look on while trying to believe that indeed no condition is permanent. Thank goodness I have got over the self-pity despite the daily humiliation of not being able to look after myself. Those first few weeks were hell, pure hell.

Now, I certainly don't wish myself dead. At least, not on most days, for even such as it is, life still has its moments, like the ones I'm enjoying right now with Linnie, standing on a stool behind the bed, busy plaiting and unplaiting my hair. I wish she could go on forever. Becky used to like playing with it when we were first married, but she gradually lost interest. Linnie's mother, Melissa, did it now and then when she was growing up, but I had a few years of being deprived of that particular pleasure until Linnie took over.

She is working with delightful concentration, even though she is regaling me with news from her school and from her family at the same time. She has already told me that yesterday Hatib drilled her in her tables up to five and gave her ten Smarties (a type of candy) when she got them all

156

right. Now I am listening to how Mamma Koso gave little Zak undiluted orange squash which "made his pooh look like orange plasticine," and how Melissa got very angry with Koso when she was so stupid and warned her that one more stupid thing like that and she would be sacked.

"Leh you nor kam kil mi pikin," Linnie says, giggling while I sigh with pleasure inside.

She is about to launch into yet another tale when Becky comes in with my mid-afternoon tablet and a drink. It's time for me to take a nap and time for Becky to help me empty my bladder. By now, Linnie knows the routine. She stops her news in mid-sentence, says, "See you, Grandpa," and runs out of the room. Bye-bye bliss until tomorrow.

****

Sleep is eluding me tonight. Perhaps it's the moonshine seeping around the edges of the curtains that's keeping me awake. As for Becky, she is out like a light, dozing and snoring a little, poor girl. I'm glad for her because she must be worn out. Looking after an invalid husband can't be easy; yet she tells me that it is a joy to do it. I don't deserve such a blessing considering the way I lost my head over Adela. Thank God she forgave me. I wonder if there are many women who would have said the same as she did, "Ben, let's forget about it. I know you love me; you just lost your bearings for a while." The funny thing is that I wasn't really in love with her when we got married, just very, very fond of her. Becky, Becky. I so wish I wasn't putting her through this ordeal. I want to move closer to her soft body, but I can't quite manage it.

Ah, yah! From the sound of the music Maria is jumping tonight. Of course, it's Friday. I can almost smell the peppered chicken. I bet Joko is sitting in his usual corner, a cigarette pinched between his thumb and forefinger, a cold beer in front of him, lost in a world of his own. I have never been quite sure whether his mind is unhinged or retarded, but he does come out with funny statements sometimes. Like the time he announced out of the blue that, "When they buried Kezia Collier, her coffin refused to enter the cemetery." Then he hummed an entire verse of "Abide with me." He obviously had funerals on the brain that night.

Patricia is also probably at the bar, lowering her dreamy eyes and showing her dimples when a cheeky customer makes some flirtatious remark. And Cosmo - that clown - who always hailed me with, "Daddy-o" and kept us in stitches with his jokes. Ah, well, I enjoyed some *good* times when I had two legs and a good brain, which was for all of sixty years. I can't complain, really, but I would give almost anything for one last rollicking session of cold beers and forgettable conversation. I wonder what that noise is. Just my imagination... Hmm, where is sleep tonight?

****

This new day brings with it the times I love and dread – physiotherapy sessions. Sometimes the pain is unbearable, which is why I dread them. Jamesina says that is because my muscles are becoming a bit tight, and that is the damage she is trying to prevent with the exercises. Bend knee, straighten, bend knee, straighten, and on and on. Then bend elbow, straighten, bend elbow, straighten; then wrist in, wrist out, wrist in, wrist out until I feel like screaming. The sessions seem to go on for hours, though they only last thirty minutes or so.

Here she comes now, warbling: "How is my best boyfriend today? Has he been good?" It always irritates me, the way Jamesina greets me in the third person; however, she's a good girl. And she gives me hope that I shall recover one day, which is why I also love physiotherapy sessions. To distract me from the pain, she gives me news of her successes, and when I moan, she tells me, "Mr. Ben, have faith. People often recover from strokes. Take heart! In a few months you will be able to move around again. Take heart." Today is different. Jamesina is quiet after her usual greeting, sighs heavily between exercises, and even loses her rhythm from time to time. I wonder what is bothering her and try to ask, but as usual now, all that emerges from my lips is gibberish, even though I am forming perfect sentences in my head. Tears of frustration sting my ears and trickle onto the pillow.

"It's all right, Mr. Ben," she says quietly when she notices. "It's all right."

More tears flow. I feel humiliated by my weakness, but I can do nothing to stop the tears.

"Jamesina is in trouble," Becky tells me later as she settles down to give me my mid-morning drink. "She and her husband were saving towards building a house, at least, Jamesina handed him her own share every month. Just by chance she discovered their Post Office Savings Book on top of the wardrobe this morning. Ben, would you believe that it had only *one* deposit in it made *two* years ago! It's a good thing he's gone on trek because I'm sure she would have strangled him. I hope she's cooled down a bit by the time he returns. How will she handle it? I wonder. Can you

159

imagine?" I make a sound, trying to convey the idea that I am as shocked as she is by the behaviour of Jamesina's husband, but she doesn't understand what I'm trying to say. "Are you all right, darling?' she asks.

We have developed a code. Thumb down for "no" and thumb up for "yes." I raise the thumb on my good hand, and Becky smiles lovingly as she rises to her feet.

"Let me go and make lunch for Linnie," she says. "She'll soon be here."

Ah, Linnie! The light of my life! I can't wait to feel her delicate little fingers in my hair again. Her voice falls sweetly on my ears as she says, "Grandpa, good afternoon."

Thank goodness we live so close to her school; otherwise, she would have been going straight home to Mamma Koso instead of coming here to wait for Melissa, and I would have been deprived of this pleasure. Come to think of it, I wonder if Becky and Melissa decided between them that Linnie should come here every day just to cheer me up. It doesn't matter. I move my head towards her for a kiss, which she places warmly on my cheek. Bless her little heart! She never seems to notice how lopsided my face is or that I am dribbling a little. At least she doesn't comment on it.

She starts to work on my hair and I surrender to bliss once more. Presently she says, "Grandpa, today a boy peed in class. He was fighting with another boy, and Auntie Viola made them stand in a corner. They were not allowed to talk, so he could not tell her he wanted to pee. When he could not keep it any longer, he peed in the corner. Then, Auntie Viola spanked him. Do you think that was right, Grandpa?"

I am saying to myself, Hatib and Melissa are going to have problems with this one. She's a smart cookie. Linnie knows the code, so I give her the thumbs down to show that I do not approve of Auntie Viola's behaviour.

"And," she goes on, "Auntie Viola made him sit with his wet pants until the end of school."

What! A woman like that has no business working with small children, I say to myself. I make the thumbs down sign again, thinking that Hatib and Melissa ought to put Linnie in another school. If only I could talk. I would suggest that to them. If *only* I could talk. I would resign myself to losing the use of my arm and leg for the rest of my life, if only I could talk... Sensing my unhappiness, Linnie proceeds to undo the plaits she has made, comb my hair, and pat it down gently all over my head, the way she plays with dolls. Becky enters the room with my tablet and drink. And so it goes...Hmm.

Sheikh Umar Kamarah

THE TRAP

A long, long time ago, there lived an old woman in a farm house, miles away from surrounding villages, in a country called Sierra Lyoa. She lived in a seclusion of some kind. Her only company were her farm animals: Cow, Goat, and Cock. She kept a fabulous garden near the farmhouse from which she got fresh fruits and vegetables. It was a peaceful life the old woman lived. She would tend the garden regularly, as work in the garden was her only form of exercise. Ya Yenoh, the old woman, had lived in the farmhouse for over three decades. Her children, living in different parts of the world, would come to visit from time to time.

Over the years, Sierra Lyoa had been struggling with the effect of a serious drought. The farmers had been seriously hit as their rice and peanut farms could not yield anything. But Ya Yenoh's garden flourished. Everyone who visited her wondered what the old woman was doing differently. The drought had an impact even on the animals in the bush. There was a tiny animal that lived near the old woman's farmhouse. His name was rat. Rat had travelled the length and breadth of the country looking for food, but could not find any. One day, Rat was taking a casual walk near Ya Yenoh's house when he stumbled upon the old woman's garden. He found a cool area where he sat and ate whatever he could find. He returned to the bush after filling up his stomach. Since then the Rat would come regularly to eat in the garden. The old woman noticed that her crops were being stolen but could not figure out who was doing this. When she could not take it anymore, the old woman decided to set a trap in the garden. One morning, just when Rat was getting ready to go to the garden, he saw Ya Yenoh setting up a trap on one of the potato beds. He watched from the nearby bush and realized that the garden had become dangerous for thieves. Rat stayed away from the garden for a couple of days. After debating in his mind what course to take, he concluded that he should meet the old woman's farm friends, Cow, Goat, and Cock, to enlist their support to convince the old woman to disconnect the trap.

The next morning, Rat went to talk to Cow.

He began, "Good morning, Cow, I have come to discuss a serious issue with you. This concerns all of us. There is a disguised trap in the garden. I believe it is a threat to everyone, including you and me. Although I live in that bush over there, I am your friend, an animal like you. I want us to meet the old woman and plead with her to disconnect the trap."

The Cow replied, "Rat, traps are not my problem. Don't you see my neck, it is not meant for that funny instrument you call trap. I do not care whether it is there or not, and I will not talk to the old woman about it. Bye-bye."

Rat was disappointed, but he decided to try talking to Goat. He went to Goat in the afternoon and said,

"Good afternoon, Goat, I have come to you this afternoon to discuss something that concerns you and me. There is a trap in the old woman's garden. Any of us can unintentionally be caught by that trap. I would like us to meet Ya Yenoh and plead with her to disconnect the trap."

Goat smiled and said to Rat, "My friend, you certainly are not serious. Do you want me to leave my rich grass here to talk to Ya Yenoh to disconnect a trap? The trap is not my worry, please leave me alone."

By this time Rat's enthusiasm had dwindled. If he could only get one of Ya Yenoh's farm friends to go with him, the old woman might agree to disconnect the trap. "Will Cock agree with me?" Rat asked himself. "If Cock rejects my proposal, what next?" Rat wonders. He summoned enough courage to face Cock that evening. On meeting Cock, Rat said,

"Good evening, Cock; I am here this evening to discuss an issue that touches you and me, and everyone else around here. There is a disguised trap in the garden. It is a threat to any one of us. I would like you to go with me to the old woman to plead with her to disconnect the trap. Would you do that?" Cock looked at the Rat with amazement. He said to him,

"I don't understand what you are talking about. Don't you see that the garden is not my problem? I don't need to go there to get my food. As long as Ya Yenoh eats rice, I am fine. Your trap story is your headache. Go solve it yourself."

Having failed to convince anyone about the danger posed by the trap, Rat kept off the garden for a while. He thought about different ways to circumvent the trap, but none was worth trying.

One sunny afternoon, Cobra, a poisonous snake, was strolling through the old woman's garden when he walked right into the trap. He struggled, and struggled, and struggled to release himself but failed. Then he stumbled upon an idea. He thought to himself,

"It would make sense to feign death in this situation. Someone will then come and release me thinking I am dead."

Cobra recoiled into a seemingly harmless mass. That afternoon, Ya Yenoh came to the garden to pick some potato leaves to prepare her lunch. As she picked the leaves, she moved from one potato bed to another. On one of these beds lay Cobra. She did not see Cobra as her eyes were on the leaves. She unknowingly stepped on Cobra's head. The furious snake drove his poisonous teeth into the old lady's foot. The snake's poison ran into the old woman's blood stream with tremendous speed. In less than two minutes the old woman lay dead on the potato bed. News of the death of Ya Yenoh spread to the surrounding villages like wild fire in the dry season. In less than an hour, hundreds of people gathered in the farmhouse.

She was a well-known woman survived by ten sons and ten daughters, all of whom lived in distant places. Messengers were dispatched to all the children. The children and the in-laws came to pay their last respects to the old woman. As was the custom, plenty of food and drink had to be provided for the sympathizers, family friends, and others.

The eldest son suggested that Cow be slaughtered as a lot of meat would be needed for the occasion. Ten able-bodied men were assigned the task of slaughtering Cow. Cow was confronted, knocked down, and had his fore and hind legs tied. Rat was watching all of this from the nearby bush. From his position, Cow could see Rat, and Rat could see him too. He beckoned to Rat for help. Rat came near and said to Cow,

"Cow, you know I cannot come out for these people to see me. They will eat me too. This is the time for them to eat us. Do you now see how the trap was your concern too? It was the trap that caught the snake which killed the old woman; and it is the old woman's funeral that has sanctioned your death."

Then, came the fortieth-day ceremony. This was the most important occasion for the dead. It was the time for people to pay the very last respects to the dead in an elaborate way. So, the children, friends, and other relatives all came to the ceremony. Again it was time for plenty of food and drink. This time it was Goat's turn. Before he was slaughtered, he saw Rat in the nearby bush and called for help. Rat told him that he could not help him because the humans would eat him too. But he reminded Goat that it was the trap in the old woman's garden that had caused all this.

"Goat," Rat said, "do you remember the trap I talked to you about? Well, you would not be in this predicament if you had listened to me, and worked with me."

Goat did not respond.

There was an important In-Law who came from afar and so could not be there on time for the ceremony. By the time he arrived, all the food was gone. One of the women remembered that the old woman had a cock. It was Cock's turn. Before he was killed, he saw Rat in the nearby bush and beckoned to him for help. Rat replied, "You know I cannot come to the open; the humans are going to eat me. Funerals are their excuse to kill us. How I wish you had listened to me. It is that trap I talked to you about that has engulfed all of you in a web of death."

SIERRA LEONEAN WRITERS SERIES

Focusing on academic, fictional, and scientific writing that will complement other relevant materials used in schools, colleges, universities and other tertiary institutions, the Sierra Leonean Writers Series (SLWS) aims to promote good quality books by Sierra Leoneans, writers of Sierra Leonean descent from around the world, and writers writing on or about Sierra Leone. Even if the initial readership is made up of people outside Sierra Leone, it is the publisher's hope that students and other readers in Sierra Leone will eventually be at least some of the primary beneficiaries of these new works. Not only will people in Sierra Leone be able to read materials that relate to their own lives and experiences, budding writers will also be able to draw inspiration from the efforts of their compatriots and other established writers.

Submitted work undergoes a rigorous peer review process before being accepted for publication, with an international editorial board providing guidance to writers.

For further information, please visit our website:
www.sl-writers-series.org

Prof. Osman Sankoh (Mallam O.)
Publisher, SLWS
publisher@sl-writers-series.org

Ms Fatmata Sankoh
Business Manager, SLWS
Fatmata.Sankoh@sl-writers-series.org
Writersseries.sl@gmail.com

Published Books

A. History and Political Science
SLWS H&PS-1
Joe A. D. Alie, 2007
ISBN: 3-9808084-5-9
Sierra Leone Since Independence – History of a Postcolonial State
A stimulating and informative account of Sierra Leone's political history from the last years of British colonial rule to the present. The book discusses some of the forces that have tended to unite and disintegrate the nation, paying particular attention to the deeds and misdeeds of the political elite. It concludes with an analysis of the major challenges facing Sierra Leone in the post-conflict period, as well as the prospects for building a progressive, democratic, peaceful and viable nation-state.

B. CREATIVE WRITING SERIES
SLWS CW-1
Osman A. Sankoh, 2001
ISBN: 3-00-003978-3
Hybrid Eyes – An African in Europe
This semi-autobiography critically examines the experiences of Africans and other minority communities in Germany as well as key values and stereotypes that many people in Africa hold about Europe. The author acknowledges the flaws of African culture and advances proposals for the way ahead.

SLWS CW-2
Sheikh Umarr Kamarah, 2002
ISBN: 3-9808084-0-8
Singing in Exile and The Child of War
This collection of poems examines the causes of the African
(Sierra Leonean) condition, evaluates the African
immigrant's situation in the West, hints at the role and
culpability of corporate West in African wars and woes, and
concludes that African must ultimately assume the
responsibility of rebuilding their continent.

SLWS CW-3
Abdul B. Kamara, 2003
Unknown Destination
ISBN: 3-9808084-1-6
The book examines a wide spectrum of challenges that
confronted African students in the aftermath of the
economic reforms or structural adjustments of the 1980s,
and the concomitant hardship that swept across Africa.
The author uses his own real life-experiences to compare
student life in the East as experienced in China, with that
in the West (Germany), and adroitly analyses what these
unforeseen cultural divergences implied for young
Africans in search of higher education.

SLWS CW-4
Samuel Hinton, 2003
The Road to Kenema
ISBN: 3-9808084-3-2
In *The Road To Kenema* Samuel Hinton presents a poignant,
sometimes searing portrait of a man who stands with one
foot planted firmly in the ageless soil of Africa, the other on
the promise-filled shores of America. Balancing memories

of his homeland with dreams of his adopted country, Hinton takes his reader on a journey that is often upsetting, but always engaging. Each poem beckons, almost forces, the reader to experience the situation at hand...

SLWS CW-5
Karamoh Kabba, 2005
Morquee – The Political Drama of Wish over Wisdom
ISBN: 3-9808084-4-0
Morquee traces Sierra Leone's turbulent recent history through the eyes of one of the individuals caught up in it. With its patient description of how an innocent young man can become tangled in a web of corruption, deceit and war, *Morquee* is a microcosm of the post-colonial experience in much of West Africa. *Morquee* is part of a renaissance in Sierra Leonean story-telling. The Sierra Leonean Writers Series is at the forefront of this movement. With this publication, Karamoh Kabba cements his status as a bright young hope for the Sierra Leonean novel. Home-grown creativity in Sierra Leone is on the rise again.

SLWS CW-6
Yema Lucilda Hunter, 2007
Redemption Song
ISBN: **3-980-8084-6-7**
Told partly through the diaries of Emmanuel Martin, a boy on the threshold of adulthood, ***Redemption Song*** is the story of how war came to a peaceful, if impoverished, country and tore it apart. However, as Emmanuel grows up and his life unfolds, all is not doom and gloom...

SLWS CW-7
Mohamed Combo Kamanda, 2007
The Visa
ISBN: **3-980-8084-7-5**

The Visa is a lucid, informative, educative and humorous play; it is truly a "travel ticket" into the two cultures: the Western Culture which shocks and transforms many Africans upon their arrival in Europe, and the African culture with its own uniqueness – you may call it a clash of cultures, races and value systems. The play touches on these issues in a light-hearted manner. ...

SLWS CW-8
J Sorie Conteh, 2007
In Search of Sons
ISBN: **3-980-8084-8-3**

In this book, J. Sorie Conteh tells the universal story of the preference many societies/cultures in Africa have for more sons in the family than girls. The story is set in the author's country, Sierra Leone, and tells the harrowing experience of a mother who tries to fulfil her husband's desire for more sons. She becomes pregnant but eventually dies in labour *in search of sons...*

SLWS CW-9
Michael Fayia Kallon, 2010
The Ghosts of Ngaingah
ISBN: 978-9988-1-3983-4

This is a story full of superstition, yet so credible. When a people neglect that which constitutes their collective consciousness and that which helps them to grow and prosper as a community, the negative effects are bound to hit them hard.

172

SLWS CW-10
J Sorie Conteh, 2011
Family Affairs
ISBN: 978-9988-1-3984-1
In *Family Affairs* J. Sorie Conteh returns to the fictitious
town of Talia which featured in his previous book novel, *In
Search of Sons*. Once again he has dealt with the stresses,
strains and even tragedies that can arise within families
when time-honoured beliefs and expectations are
challenged.

www.ingramcontent.com/pod-product-compliance
Lightning Source LLC
Chambersburg PA
CBHW072125170626
46813CB00004B/1701